TOXIC NO MORE

RECLAIMING YOUR LIFE FROM HARMFUL RELATIONSHIPS: STRATEGIES FOR SELF-PROTECTION AND BUILDING POSITIVE CONNECTIONS

JANET G CRUZ

Published by Unlimited Concepts, Coconut Creek, Florida.

www.publishing.uconcept.com

Book, Editing, and Cover Design by Janet M Garcia | UConceptDesigns.com

Published in the United States of America.

CONTENTS

INTRODUCTION

Sarah never realized how deeply rooted her struggles with toxic emotions were until she found herself constantly on edge, snapping at her loved ones over the smallest issues. It wasn't until her relationships began to crumble around her that she sought to understand the underlying causes of her emotional turmoil. Her journey of self-discovery led her to confront and gradually dismantle the harmful patterns that had taken hold of her life. Today, Sarah radiates a peace and confidence she thought was lost to her, embodying the profound transformation that is possible when we courageously face our inner conflicts.

My name is Janet, and I have been fascinated by the nuances of human behavior and social interactions from a young age. This curiosity propelled me to pursue degrees in psychology and sociology, fields that have equipped me with a deep understanding of the psychological and social frameworks that shape our interactions and emotional health.

This book, "Toxic No More - Reclaiming Your Life from Harmful Relationships" is constructed from a blend of personal insight, academic knowledge, and experience. It is designed to inspire hope and provide you with the tools necessary to free yourself from the grip of toxic emotions and toxic relationships. Through its pages, I aim to empower you to identify, confront, and overcome the destructive emotional patterns that hinder your personal and relational growth. It was structured to guide you through understanding the nature of toxic emotions and offers a clear path from gaining awareness to applying practical strategies that foster emotional health and build positive, supportive relationships. You can expect to find not only theoretical insights but also actionable advice that resonates with both your heart and mind.

The tone of this book is empathetic and empowering, aiming to create a supportive space where you can explore your emotions without judgment and find encouragement for your journey toward healing. This book is for you—whether you're an adult or a young adult who is looking for ways to heal and forge healthier relationships.

It is a fact that there is a strong need for resources that combine emotional depth with practical applications, and this book meets that need by addressing the emotional, psychological, and physical impacts of toxic emotions, supported by data and real-life examples.

What sets this book apart is not just the richness of its academic foundations but also its commitment to real-world applicability. I invite you to not only read but to also engage actively with the content by interlacing theory with the practical exercises provided. Through reflections and strategies outlined here, you'll be equipped to initiate meaningful changes in your life.

I encourage you to immerse yourself into the exercises and reflections provided throughout this book. Engage with them as tools that can catalyze your personal transformation and empower you to reclaim a life marked by emotional health and positive relationships.

Welcome to a journey of transformation and empowerment. Let's begin this path to becoming **Toxic No More**!

UNDERSTANDING TOXIC EMOTIONS

*H*ave you ever felt like a puppet, with strings pulled by unseen forces, dictating your every mood and reaction? This is how it feels like when living with toxic emotions—a state where persistent negative feelings control your actions and cloud your life's potential. Recognizing and managing these emotions isn't just about feeling better; it's a crucial step towards reclaiming your autonomy and building a life filled with more positive relationships and inner peace.

Toxic emotions are like weeds in the garden, but in your mind, growing wildly, often unnoticed, until they've taken over who you really are. They manifest as persistent feelings of anger, jealousy, fear, or sadness that do not just affect you momentarily; they linger, affecting your behavior, your relationships, and even your perception of the world. The first step to regaining control is to identify these emotions and understand their triggers.

DEFINING TOXIC EMOTIONS AND THEIR TRIGGERS

Think of toxic emotions as unwanted guests invading the sanctuary of your mind, often arriving without invitation and refusing to leave, turning your inner world upside down. These emotions, which include persistent forms of anger, jealousy, and fear, significantly harm your emotional health. For instance, chronic anger can strain relationships and impede communication, while enduring jealousy might prevent you from forming meaningful connections due to mistrust or insecurity. Similarly, ongoing fear can paralyze you, hindering your ability to make decisions or take risks that are necessary for personal growth.

The triggers of these toxic emotions are as varied as the emotions themselves, originating from both external and internal sources. Externally, like a stressful work environment or tumultuous personal relationships, they can precipitate feelings of anxiety or anger. Internally, like personal insecurities or unresolved trauma, can manifest as jealousy or fear. Remember Sarah, who found herself lashing out in anger at colleagues. It wasn't the immediate stresses of her job that were the root cause but an underlying fear of inadequacy that she hadn't addressed. Her perception of her colleagues as more competent triggered a defensive, angry response to conceal her insecurities.

Our perceptions play a significant role in how we experience emotions. Two individuals might face the same situation, yet their emotional responses could be completely opposite, influenced by how they perceive the event. If you perceive a friend's remark as a slight, you might feel hurt or angry, whereas another person might see it as constructive criticism and feel motivated to improve. By altering our perceptions, we can often change our emotional responses. Techniques such as cognitive reframing, where you consciously shift your perspective on a situation, can be instrumental in managing toxic emotions. For example, instead of seeing feedback as a personal attack, viewing it as an opportunity for growth can help mitigate feelings of defensiveness or resentment.

Moreover, understanding and managing toxic emotions is closely linked to the concept of emotional intelligence. Emotional intelligence involves recognizing your own emotions and those of others, discerning between different feelings, and using this information to guide your thoughts and actions. Enhancing your emotional intelligence can really empower you to handle your emotions more effectively, preventing them from gaining control over your life. It sets the foundation for more advanced strategies to manage personal and interpersonal challenges, which we'll address in subsequent chapters.

As we proceed, remember that the journey to overcoming toxic emotions is not about suppressing your feelings but understanding and redirecting them in ways that serve your well-being and promote healthier relationships. You can take the first step towards a liberated and more emotionally intelligent self by recognizing the signs of toxic emotions and learning to manage their triggers.

THE SCIENCE OF EMOTION: HOW FEELINGS AFFECT BEHAVIOR

The complex interaction of our emotions and behaviors is tied to the biology of our brains, specifically the limbic system. This area of the brain, often referred to as the emotional center of the brain, includes structures such as the amygdala, hippocampus, and hypothalamus, which together play a pivotal role in processing and regulating our emotional experiences. The amygdala, for example, is essential for emotional responses to stimuli, particularly those that might be perceived as threats. When it's activated, it triggers a chain of biological reactions designed to protect us—what we often know as the 'fight or flight' response.

This biological response system illustrates just how directly our emotions can influence our behaviors. Take fear, for instance. When you encounter something frightening, the amygdala reacts instantaneously, sending signals that increase your heart rate and blood pressure, preparing your body to either flee from the danger or confront it. This primal mechanism, while vital for survival, can also lead to avoidance behaviors if the source of fear is more psychological than physical. For example, someone who has experienced embarrassment during a public speaking may develop a deeply-rooted fear of it, leading to avoidance of any situation that requires speaking in front of an audience.

Anger, on the other hand, often leads to aggression. This emotion can activate the amygdala, prompting an adrenaline rush that prepares the body for confrontation. Even though this is a useful reaction when you face a legitimate threat, this physiological response can also lead to inappropriate or destructive behavior. Understanding this can help individuals recognize when their anger is likely to lead to aggression and develop strategies to manage their response more constructively.

The relationship between emotions and behaviors is not one-way; it forms a loop wherein each influences the other. Behavioral responses to emotions can reinforce the feelings themselves, creating cycles that can be either beneficial or harmful. For instance, if avoidance behavior reduces anxiety temporarily, the brain learns to repeat that behavior whenever anxiety arises, reinforcing the avoidance behavior. On the other hand, confronting fears can decrease the fear response over time, as *exposure therapy* (a type of therapy in which you are exposed to what you fear, like a situation, an activity, or even to some things) has shown in clinical settings.

Neuroscience and psychology research provides a vast amount of evidence supporting these connections between emotions and behaviors. Studies using brain imaging technology, such as MRIs (Functional Magnetic Resonance Imaging), have allowed scientists to observe the brain in action as it processes emotional stimuli and generates corresponding behaviors. These findings not only validate the biological basis of our emotional experiences but also highlight the plasticity of the brain—its ability to adapt based on new experiences.

Understanding this biological underpinnings of how emotions impact behavior is crucial for anyone seeking to break free from toxic emotional patterns. By recognizing the roles played by different parts of the brain in emotion regulation and behavior, you'll be able to better understand the responses to various situations and learn more effective ways to manage your emotions. This knowledge empowers you to take proactive steps towards changing the behaviors that stem from toxic emotions, setting the stage for a more conscious and controlled handling of our emotional reactions.

RECOGNIZING PATTERNS: SELF-REFLECTION ON PERSONAL EMOTIONAL TRIGGERS

The path to understanding and transforming toxic emotions starts with the recognition of the patterns these emotions often form in our lives. We must learn to identify the recurring emotional responses that signal underlying issues, just like a detective collects and pieces together clues at a crime scene. This process begins effectively with the practice of keeping an emotions diary or journal. This simple but powerful tool serves as a mirror that reflects our emotional habits back to us, providing insights that might otherwise remain obscured by the chaos of our daily life.

When structuring your emotions diary, consider logging the emotions you feel as well as the circumstances surrounding these feelings. Like: who was involved, what was happening, where and when it occurred, and any thoughts that were going through your mind at the time. For example, you might record an incident where you felt angry during a meeting at work. Detailing the specific triggers—perhaps a comment from a colleague or feeling unheard in a discussion—can help you identify patterns over time. This practice of logging and reflection doesn't just serve as a record; it's an act of mindfulness, encouraging you to live more observantly and responsively rather than reactively.

The importance of recognizing these patterns cannot be overstated. It is only by understanding the 'what' and 'why' of our emotional responses that we can begin to address and alter them. This understanding is crucial because our emotional reactions often operate automatically. They are the well-worn paths in our psychological world, formed through years of habit and, often, necessity. However, as our circumstances and understanding grow, these once useful reactions can become outdated and maladaptive, manifesting as toxic patterns that disrupt our lives and damage our relationships.

To gain a deeper understanding of these patterns, I encourage engaging in guided self-reflection exercises designed to prompt introspection. Consider questions like: What emotions do I feel most often? What times of day are these feelings most intense? Are there specific people or situations that trigger these emotions? How do I respond to these feelings internally and externally? The answers to these questions can offer profound insights into your emotional world. By regularly engaging with these reflective practices, you can start to see, not just the outlines of your emotional habits, but the shapes of your inner (deeper) self.

Awareness is the first step towards change. Once you have a clearer understanding of your emotional patterns, you can begin to take proactive steps to modify them. This doesn't mean suppressing your feelings but rather approaching them with a new perspective and toolkit. For example, if you recognize that you often respond to stress with withdrawal and silence, you might decide to try expressing your feelings in the moment or discussing them afterward as an alternative approach. This shift doesn't negate your feelings but empowers you to handle them in ways that are constructive rather than destructive.

This proactive change is not about finding quick fixes but nurturing long-lasting and sustainable growth. It's about rewriting ourselves to reflect who we are now and who we aspire to become. By recognizing and adjusting our emotional responses, we reclaim control over our emotions and, as a result, our lives. This process of self-reflection and proactive change forms the foundation upon which we can build healthier relationships with ourselves and others, fostering a life that is not just free from toxicity but rich with understanding and fulfillment.

THE PHYSICAL IMPACT OF EMOTIONAL TOXICITY

Understanding the connection between our emotional health and physical well-being is imperative, as the two are not just interconnected but deeply interdependent. Chronic toxic emotions such as prolonged stress, anxiety, and depression do not merely disrupt mental health; they have tangible effects on physical health, potentially leading to serious conditions such as heart disease, diabetes, and a weakened immune system. This realization emphasizes the importance of addressing emotional toxicity not just for mental tranquility but also for maintaining physical health.

The relationship between chronic emotional stress and physical ailments is well-documented in medical literature. For example, prolonged exposure to high levels of stress hormones like cortisol and adrenaline can be detrimental to the body. These hormones, which are part of the body's *fight-or-flight* response, are beneficial in short bursts, helping us react to immediate threats. However, when these hormone levels remain elevated due to ongoing stress or anxiety, they can lead to increased blood pressure, which over time, increases the risk of heart disease. Similarly, high cortisol levels can contribute to the buildup of fat in the abdominal area, leading to obesity and associated diseases such as type 2 diabetes. Furthermore, chronic stress impairs the immune system, making the body more susceptible to infections and slower to heal from wounds or illness.

The interconnectedness of mind and body is supported by numerous studies showing the impact of emotional health on overall well-being. Research has indicated that individuals with high levels of anxiety or depression have a significantly higher risk of developing cardiovascular and metabolic diseases. This data is a clear call to action, emphasizing the need for strategies to mitigate emotional toxicity as a preventive measure for various physical health conditions.

Addressing these issues requires more than temporary fixes; it demands lifestyle adjustments that foster both mental and physical health. Regular physical exercise, for instance, is one of the most effective ways to reduce stress. Activities like walking, jogging, or yoga not only help in reducing the levels of stress hormones but also stimulate the production of *endorphins*, chemicals in the brain that act as natural painkillers and mood elevators. Integrating regular exercise into your daily routine can be a powerful tool in maintaining emotional balance and physical health.

Another significant adjustment involves the practice of meditation or mindfulness techniques. These practices help in managing stress by focusing the mind on the present moment and reducing the tendency to ruminate on past events or worry about the future, which are common triggers for stress and anxiety. Regular meditation has been shown to lower cortisol levels, improve immune function, and enhance overall well-being.

Diet also plays a crucial role in managing emotional and physical health. Consuming a balanced diet rich in fruits, vegetables, lean proteins, and whole grains provides the necessary nutrients that support brain function and, by extension, emotional regulation. Additionally, certain foods like fatty fish, which are high in omega-3 fatty acids, have been shown to reduce the symptoms of depression and anxiety. Conversely, a diet high in refined sugars and unhealthy fats can exacerbate these symptoms, as well as contribute to physical health issues like obesity and heart disease.

Incorporating these lifestyle changes requires commitment and consistency, but the benefits they bring to both emotional and physical health are invaluable. As we continue to explore the profound effects of emotions on our body, it becomes increasingly clear that fostering emotional health is inextricably linked to leading a healthier, happier life. By adopting healthier lifestyle choices, we not only improve our mood and mental health but also fortify our bodies against the physical manifestations of emotional toxicity.

PSYCHOLOGICAL THEORIES BEHIND EMOTIONAL TOXICITY

To fully understand emotional toxicity, it is important to examine theories that not only clarify the origin and perpetuation of these harmful emotions, but also provide ways for healing and growth. Cognitive Behavioral Therapy (CBT) and Dialectical Behavior Therapy (DBT) are two such frameworks that have proven highly effective in helping people cope with a wide range of emotional difficulties.

Cognitive Behavioral Therapy proposes that our thoughts, feelings, and behaviors are interconnected, and that negative thought patterns, which CBT calls 'cognitive distortions', can lead to emotional distress. Cognitive distortions are essentially ways in which our mind convinces us of something that isn't really true. These inaccurate thoughts are usually used to reinforce negative thinking or emotions — telling ourselves things that sound rational and accurate, but really only serve to keep us feeling bad about ourselves. For example, a person might believe, "If I do not succeed in my tasks, I am a failure." This kind of all-or-nothing thinking, where no middle ground exists, will elevate stress significantly and hinder performance. CBT works by helping individuals identify their distortions, challenge these false beliefs, and replace them with more objective, realistic and positive thoughts, thereby decreasing emotional distress and self-destructive behavior.

Dialectical Behavior Therapy, on the other hand, is particularly effective for those who experience emotions very intensely. It is a form of therapy specifically designed to help people change patterns of behavior that are not helpful, such as self-harm, suicidal thinking, and substance abuse. This approach works on the premise that some people react in a more intense and out-of-the-ordinary manner toward certain emotional situations, primarily those found in romantic, family, and friend relationships. DBT introduces the concept of dialectics or the process of synthesizing opposing viewpoints to find a balance between acceptance and change. One of its fundamental principles is mindfulness, which is about being fully aware and present in the moment. By practicing mindfulness, you can learn to accept your feelings, yourself, and your situations as they are.

These psychological theories also examine how our emotional development is influenced by our early life experiences. It is widely recognized that our childhood and upbringing play a pivotal role in forming our emotional responses as adults. For instance, if a child is frequently criticized or punished, they may develop a propensity to perceive many future interactions as critical or punishing, even when they are not. This can lead to a constant state of fear or defensiveness, which might manifest in toxic behaviors such as passive aggression or withdrawal in relationships. Both CBT and DBT work through these issues by helping individuals understand the origins of their emotional responses and by providing them with tools to reshape these learned patterns of thinking and behaving.

To illustrate the effectiveness of these therapies, consider the case study of a young woman named Lisa. Lisa dealt with severe anxiety and mistrust in relationships due to early parental instability and conflict. Through CBT, she learned to recognize and reframe her belief that "all relationships are doomed to fail", a belief that was rooted in her since childhood. By challenging this distortion and practicing new ways of thinking, Lisa was able to foster healthier relationships and reduce her anxiety. Similarly, in another instance, a man named Mark benefited from DBT after a history of impulsive behaviors and substance abuse. Through skills learned in DBT, such as emotional regulation and mindfulness, he was able to gain greater control over his actions and emotional responses, leading to improved personal and professional relationships.

These therapies underscore the transformative power of understanding and actively reshaping our psychological perspective.

By engaging with these therapeutic approaches, individuals who suffer from the effects of toxic emotions can find viable pathways to healing and ultimately, lead more fulfilled and less burdened lives. Whether it's through identifying distorted thinking with CBT or balancing acceptance and change with DBT, the journey towards emotional health is both possible and promising. With the guidance of these psychological theories, we can maneuver through our complex emotions and emerge with a stronger, more resilient sense of self.

TOXICITY WITHIN RELATIONSHIPS

*T*oxic relationships can shroud your life's path in shadow, making it difficult to move forward or see clearly, just as when you're walking through a dense forest and the sun can't shine through. These relationships, characterized by patterns of behavior that undermine your well-being, can have profound effects on your emotions. Identifying and understanding the nature of these relationships is crucial for anyone looking to bring light back into their life and clear the way for healthier interactions.

IDENTIFYING TOXIC RELATIONSHIPS IN YOUR LIFE

Toxic relationships often manifest through subtle signs that might not be immediately apparent. One of the most telling signs is a consistent lack of support. In a healthy relationship, whether it's romantic, familial, or professional, support plays a foundational role. It involves the mutual exchange of encouragement, comfort, and respect for each other's autonomy and dreams. In contrast, toxic relationships are marked by a one-sidedness where the support flows in only one direction, leaving you drained and unsupported.

Persistent negativity is another red flag. This can range from constant criticism and belittlement to more passive behaviors like perpetual pessimism or discouragement from pursuing new ideas or ambitions. This relentless negativity not only saps your energy but can also start to color your view of yourself and your capabilities, leading to decreased self-esteem and emotional instability.

Feelings of being emotionally drained after interactions are a key indicator of a toxic relationship. Healthy interactions energize you; they leave you feeling better off than before. If you consistently feel worse, it's a sign that the relationship is taking more from you than it's giving. Non-reciprocal interactions, where one party consistently benefits at the other's expense, are a hallmark of such draining, unhealthy relationships.

Recognizing these signs is the first step in addressing the toxicity. To aid in this self-assessment, consider using tools like relationship quizzes* that evaluate various aspects of your interactions with others. These can help you identify patterns that may indicate toxicity in friendships, romantic relationships, or even professional connections. By reflecting on questions about reciprocity, support, respect, and personal feelings

---

* https://empathi.com/blog/top-5-science-based-relationship-quizzes/

post-interactions, you can begin to map out the nature of your relationships and discern which ones may be harmful.

The emotional impact of remaining in toxic relationships can be deep and far-reaching. Over time, the persistent negativity, lack of support, and emotional drainage can erode your self-esteem and destabilize your emotional health. This erosion can manifest in feelings of worthlessness, insecurity, and helplessness, which may pervade all areas of life, from personal aspirations to professional endeavors.

If you find that one or more of your relationships exhibit these toxic traits, taking initial steps towards change is crucial. Setting boundaries is often an effective first response. This involves clearly communicating your needs and limits to the other person. For instance, if constant criticism is an issue, you might need to assertively state that while constructive feedback is welcome, negative comments that serve no purpose but to belittle will no longer be tolerated.

Seeking external advice can also provide valuable perspective and guidance. Whether it's from a therapist, a trusted mentor, or a support group, external input can help you see solutions and alternatives that may not be apparent from within the situation. This outside perspective can be instrumental in helping you navigate your way out of the toxicity and towards healthier, more fulfilling relationships.

Personal Reflection Exercise

To further assist in your self-assessment and to encourage active engagement with this process, here is a simple exercise:

Reflect on a recent interaction in a relationship you suspect might be toxic. Write down how the interaction made you feel, what was said, and how both parties behaved. Then, assess this interaction against the signs of toxicity discussed: Was there support? Was the interaction reciprocal? How did you feel afterward? This exercise not only aids in recognizing toxic patterns but also serves as a practice in mindfulness, enhancing your awareness in future interactions.

UNDERSTANDING MANIPULATIVE BEHAVIORS AND GASLIGHTING

Manipulation and gaslighting are terms often heard in discussions about toxic relationships, yet their meanings and implications can sometimes blur. Manipulation in relationships involves one person exerting control over another through deceptive or indirect tactics rather than open communication. These tactics can range from subtle suggestions and passive-aggressive comments to more overt forms of coercion. Gaslighting, a specific type of manipulation, occurs when one person tries to convince another to doubt their perceptions, memories, or sanity, often by denying factual information, lying, or contradicting. This can lead the victim to question their reality, which is precisely the manipulator's goal.

The psychological impact of these behaviors on the victim can be profound and debilitating. Often, victims of manipulation and gaslighting experience a significant erosion of confidence, as they are repeatedly told that their views or memories are incorrect or that their feelings are irrational. This constant doubt can lead to a state of confusion and emotional instability, making it difficult for victims to make decisions or trust their judgment. Over time, this can escalate into a dependency on the manipulator for validation and reality-checking, which only serves to entrench the toxic dynamic further.

To counteract manipulation and gaslighting, it is imperative to develop communication techniques and mental strategies that reinforce personal boundaries and self-trust. One effective strategy is the use of assertive communication, where you express your thoughts and feelings openly and honestly, without aggression. When you suspect manipulation, assertively stating your perspective and refusing to engage in debates about your sanity or perceptions can help to disrupt the manipulative cycle. For instance, you might say, "I understand your perspective, but my experience of the situation is different," which acknowledges the other person's view without undermining your own.

Another critical strategy is to maintain a personal record of events or conversations when you feel gaslighting might be occurring. Keeping a journal, as mentioned before, where you can document your experiences and feelings can help you preserve your reality and serve as a reference to confirm the accuracy of your memories. This practice can be particularly empowering in moments of doubt and can provide a solid ground from which to assert your perspective.

Real-life examples further illustrate how these strategies can be implemented effectively. Consider the case of Emily, who began to notice that her partner often contradicted her memories of events, suggesting she was remembering them wrong. This led to her questioning her sanity until she started keeping a detailed journal. With the evidence in hand, she was able to confront her partner more confidently and eventually sought therapy to strengthen her ability to trust her perceptions. In another scenario, Michael found himself frequently yielding to his boss's demands, which often felt unreasonable. By adopting assertive communication techniques, he began to set clear boundaries at work, expressing his capacity and limitations openly, which not only reduced his stress but also improved the respect his boss had for him.

These stories demonstrate the effectiveness of assertive communication and reality-confirmation strategies in dealing with manipulative behaviors. By staying true to your experiences and communicating your boundaries clearly, you can begin to dismantle the dynamics of manipulation and gaslighting, paving the way for healthier, more respectful relationships.

THE ROLE OF DEPENDENCY IN TOXIC RELATIONSHIPS

Dependency, whether emotional or financial, forms complex connections in the dynamics of many toxic relationships. Emotional dependency occurs when someone relies excessively on another person to supply their emotional needs, such as validation, companionship, and security. This form of dependency often develops from feelings of insecurity or inadequacy, where the dependent person believes they cannot find contentment or safety on their own. Financial dependency adds another layer, occurring when one partner relies on the other for financial support to a degree that limits their autonomy. This kind of dependency not only binds the dependent person to the relationship but also diminishes their ability to make independent life choices, as their financial wellbeing is tied directly to the relationship.

Dependency frequently originates from a lack of self-esteem and self-worth, which runs deep within a person. When individuals doubt their value or question their capabilities, they are more likely to cling to others who appear to offer strength or stability, even when such relationships are unhealthy. This attachment is not merely a preference but feels like a necessity for those with diminished self-worth, making the idea of leaving a toxic relationship not only discouraging but, in their eyes, unfeasible. They might fear that without the relationship, they would be unable to cope or function, despite the pain or distress the relationship causes.

Breaking free from dependency requires a multifaceted approach, starting with the strengthening of one's sense of self. This can often involve learning new skills or diving into personal development areas that foster a greater sense of competence and self-reliance. For instance, someone who has relied on their partner to manage finances might benefit from financial courses or budgeting workshops, gaining skills that boost their confidence in managing their own money. Similarly, taking up new hobbies or returning to neglected interests can provide not only a sense of accomplishment but also sources of joy and fulfillment that are independent of any relationship.

Expanding one's social network also plays a crucial role in overcoming dependency. A robust network can provide emotional support and validation, reducing the reliance on a single individual to fulfill these needs. Engaging in community activities, joining clubs or groups that align with one's interests, or even volunteering can open opportunities to connect with others and build supportive, enriching friendships. These relationships can offer not only companionship but also perspectives and advice from those who might have faced similar challenges.

Professional counseling is another valuable resource in addressing and overcoming dependency. Therapists can help individuals understand the roots of their dependency, develop strategies to build self-esteem, and learn healthier ways to relate to others. Counseling provides a safe space to explore one's feelings and fears about leaving a toxic relationship, bolstered by the guidance of someone with expertise in navigating such complex emotional areas.

The benefits of gaining independence are profound and far-reaching. With increased independence, mental health tends to improve as individuals feel more in control of their lives and less at the mercy of another's whims or moods. Decision-making also improves as one gains confidence in their judgment and abilities, free from the overshadowing opinions or desires of a controlling partner. Perhaps most importantly, independence opens the door to healthier relationships. When individuals can enter relationships from a position of strength and self-sufficiency, they are better equipped to establish boundaries, communicate their needs, and engage in mutually supportive partnerships where both parties contribute and benefit equally.

As you reflect on your relationships and consider your own experiences with dependency, remember that the journey to independence is challenging but rewarding. It is a path marked by personal growth, self-discovery, and, ultimately, a deeper and more resilient sense of self.

WHEN TO RECOGNIZE A RELATIONSHIP IS BEYOND REPAIR

At times, the damage within a relationship accumulates to such an extent that the possibility of mending it becomes remote. Recognizing when a relationship has reached this point is crucial for your emotional well-being. Certain situations and behaviors, such as ongoing abuse, persistent dishonesty, or any actions that compromise your safety, are clear indicators that a relationship may be beyond repair. Abuse, whether emotional, physical, or psychological, fundamentally erodes trust and respect, which are the cornerstones of any healthy relationship. Similarly, chronic dishonesty, where lies and deceit become a routine, disrupts the foundation of trust to a degree that often cannot be restored. When your safety— emotional or physical—is at risk, the environment becomes toxic, making it not only unhealthy but potentially dangerous to remain in such a relationship.

Deciding to end a relationship, especially one that has been a significant part of your life, involves a complex interplay of emotions and practical considerations. The decision-making process is rarely straightforward and is often accompanied by a range of emotions from relief to grief. It's important to assess not only your feelings but also the tangible aspects of your life that will be impacted by this change. Questions such as "Can I support myself financially?" or "What will my social life look like after this relationship?" are important to consider. It's also important to evaluate the potential benefits of leaving, such as the possibility of a healthier, happier existence, free from the chaos that has characterized the relationship.

The support of professionals and your friends or family is extremely valuable during this emotional turmoil. Participating in therapy sessions can provide you with a structured environment to explore your feelings, receive unbiased feedback, and develop strategies for handling the transition. Support groups offer the chance to connect with others who have been through similar experiences, providing a sense of community and understanding. Additionally, leaning on trusted friends and family can give you the emotional support you need to navigate this challenging period. They can offer help, like a place to stay, or emotional support, such as being a listening ear when you need to talk.

Moving forward from a broken relationship involves both emotional closure and practical steps to rebuild your life. Emotional closure is a personal process, where you come to terms with the end of the relationship and all that it entails. This might involve practices like writing a farewell letter that you never send or more formal goodbyes, which can facilitate a sense of finality. Practical steps might include disentangling your shared assets, moving to a new living space, or even starting new traditions that reinforce your new beginning. It's also important to allow yourself time to grieve the loss of the relationship while gradually starting to fill your life with activities and people that reinforce your independence and self-worth. This dual approach ensures that you are not only moving past the relationship but are also moving toward something new and hopeful.

STRATEGIES FOR HANDLING TOXIC FAMILY DYNAMICS

Dealing with toxic family relationships can be especially difficult or challenging because of the strong ties and long-standing responsibilities that typically define these connections. Unlike other types of relationships, family ties form part of our lives from birth; they are imbued with expectations, histories, and emotional complexities that can make toxicity very difficult to manage. The stakes are high, and the emotional terrain is intricate, as these relationships play critical roles in shaping our identities and our views on love and security.

I can't emphasize enough how complicated it is to set up boundaries within such dynamics. It involves a delicate balance of asserting your needs while maintaining respect for family bonds. The problem is that even if you set the boundaries, chances are that other family members won't respect that.

The first step in this process is often the hardest—clearly defining what your boundaries are. This could be deciding not to discuss certain topics that lead to conflict, such as politics, religion or lifestyle choices, or limiting the frequency of contact with family members who drain your emotional reserves. Communicating these boundaries is equally important. Use clear, assertive communication to express your needs without blame or guilt. For instance, you might say, "I value our time together, but I need to step back from conversations about my career choices to maintain my well-being." It's essential to be consistent in enforcing these boundaries, as inconsistency can send mixed signals that may lead to boundary violations.

Maintaining personal integrity in the face of toxic family dynamics involves staying true to your values and beliefs, even when they might conflict with those of your family. This can be challenging, especially when faced with intense pressure or criticism. Your family means well but their approach may be incorrect. However, anchoring yourself in your personal values will help in guiding your interactions and decisions, helping to preserve your sense of self. It's helpful to regularly reflect on what is most important to you and why, reaffirming your commitment to these values in your daily life. This practice not only strengthens your resolve but also builds self-respect, which is essential for healthy self-esteem.

Coping with unavoidable interactions, such as during family gatherings or holidays, requires practical strategies to manage stress and maintain composure. One effective approach is to plan ahead, anticipating potential stressors and preparing responses or actions to mitigate them. For example, if certain topics of conversation are known triggers (Ej. religion), plan polite but firm ways to steer the conversation elsewhere, or have an exit strategy to take a break from the interaction.

Another strategy is to set time limits for your participation in potentially stressful family interactions, which can provide a sense of control and reduce feelings of being trapped. Additionally, focusing on self-care before and after such gatherings can help manage stress. Engaging in activities that relax and recharge you, such as reading, yoga, or spending time with supportive friends, can fortify your emotional resilience.

When managing toxic family dynamics, it's imperative to recognize that while you can strive for healthier interactions, you cannot control the behaviors or reactions of others. This understanding can alleviate frustration and lead to a more accepting attitude towards the complexities of family relationships, promoting emotional well-being despite any challenge.

Getting through the complexities of toxic family dynamics is a journey marked by challenges and learning. It requires a delicate balance of assertiveness, compassion, and resilience. Setting clear boundaries, maintaining personal integrity. Practicing the coping strategies mentioned earlier not only will protect your emotional health but also pave the way for healthier interactions in the future.

BUILDING EMOTIONAL RESILIENCE

*O*ur emotional world is similar to when you throw a pebble on a lake, creating ripples that expand gradually disrupting the calm waters and slowly dissipates. In the same way, your emotional world, which is mostly calm, will be occasionally disturbed by challenges and stressors. Building emotional resilience is akin to preparing your emotional lake for those pebbles, ensuring that the ripples disturb as little as possible and recover more quickly. In this chapter, we will explore how to fortify your emotional boundaries.

TECHNIQUES FOR STRENGTHENING EMOTIONAL BOUNDARIES

Defining Emotional Boundaries

Emotional boundaries are like invisible lines we draw around our feelings and responsibilities, determining what we are comfortable with and how we allow others to treat us. Just as a fence around a property dictates who can enter and what belongs within its perimeter, emotional boundaries help guard your mental space against unwanted intrusions and demands. These boundaries are crucial not just for your emotional health but also for nurturing relationships based on mutual respect and understanding.

However, establishing and maintaining healthy boundaries is not always intuitive. It often requires conscious effort and understanding, especially for those who have grown accustomed to putting others' needs before their own. If you find yourself frequently overwhelmed by others' demands or struggling to voice your needs, it's likely that your emotional boundaries need some attention.

Identifying Signs of Weak Boundaries

One of the clearest signs of weak emotional boundaries is the feeling of being overwhelmed by others' needs and emotions. If you often find yourself saying yes when you desperately want to say no, or if you feel guilty for asserting your preferences, these are indicators that your boundaries might be too porous. Another symptom is the feeling of being taken advantage of, or a chronic sense of dissatisfaction in your relationships, suggesting that your boundaries are not effectively protecting your emotional well-being.

Strategies for Boundary-Setting

Setting boundaries involves clear communication and self-awareness. You can begin by identifying areas where your boundaries are constantly being challenged. Is it at work, where colleagues might be dumping responsibilities on you? Or in personal relationships, where your time and energy are not being respected? Take a moment to think about this.

Once identified, the next step is to communicate these boundaries clearly. This doesn't have to be confrontational. In fact, it can be done with kindness and assertiveness. For example, if a friend has a habit of calling late at night to vent, you might say, "I care about what's going on with you, but I need to turn off my phone at 10 PM to ensure I get enough sleep. Can we find a better time to discuss this?"

Role-playing can be a useful tool to practice setting boundaries. Imagine different scenarios where your boundaries could be challenged, and rehearse how you would respond. This preparation can make you feel more confident in handling real-life situations.

Maintaining Boundaries

Being consistent to maintain your boundaries is as important as setting those boundaries. Be prepared for some pushback; it's natural for others to resist and test limits, especially if they're used to a certain dynamic. Stay firm and remember that maintaining your boundaries is not just about protecting yourself, but also about fostering healthier interactions with others. It will take some time for others to adjust to your change.

You must handle each boundary violation effectively if you want them to remain. If someone repeatedly disrespects your boundaries, it may be necessary to reevaluate and possibly limit the level of interaction you have with them. Communicate the specific boundary that has been crossed and the impact it has had on you, reinforcing your expectations for future interactions.

For instance, if a colleague continues to delegate their tasks to you despite your clear communication, you might need to escalate the matter by involving a supervisor or HR. This action reaffirms your boundaries and shows that you are serious about maintaining them.

Incorporating these strategies into your daily life will not only strengthen your emotional resilience but also empower you to build and sustain healthier, more respectful relationships. As you practice these techniques, remember that setting and maintaining boundaries is an ongoing process that requires patience and persistence. However, the peace and empowerment that come from having strong emotional boundaries are well worth the effort.

RESILIENCE TRAINING: BUILDING YOUR EMOTIONAL MUSCLE

Resilience training is akin to strengthening your emotional core, much like physical training enhances your body's capability to withstand stress and recover quicker. Emotional resilience, in its essence, is about developing your ability to bounce back from setbacks and stress, maintaining a stable equilibrium amid life's inevitable ups and downs. Think of it as increasing your emotional buffer, allowing you to handle pressures and recover more quickly from difficulties.

To build this kind of resilience, it will be beneficial to engage in specific exercises that fortify your emotional robustness. *Visualization techniques* are particularly effective. For example, imagine a scenario in which you are faced with a significant challenge—perhaps delivering a presentation at work. Visualize yourself handling the situation with confidence and poise, navigating any difficulties with calm and assurance. This mental rehearsal can significantly enhance your real-world performance, as it primes your mind to act in ways that reflect the successful outcomes you've envisioned.

Another resilience-building exercise involves *scenario planning*. This technique requires you to think through a potential stressor or challenge and plan out various ways to cope with it. By doing so, you prepare yourself to face and manage the situation effectively, reducing anxiety and enhancing confidence. For instance, if you're concerned about a forthcoming job interview, you could outline several possible outcomes and strategies for each, such as questions you might be asked and how you would answer them. This preparation not only alleviates stress but also improves your adaptability and problem-solving skills in real-time situations.

Resilience drills can also be incorporated into your routine. These could involve setting small, daily challenges for yourself and then reflecting on how you managed them. Over time, this practice builds a 'muscle memory' of sorts for resilience, making you better equipped to handle larger challenges as they arise. For instance, you might decide to tackle a small project you've been postponing. As you complete these daily challenges and reflect on your successes and areas for improvement, you gradually enhance your ability to cope with more significant stressors.

The connection between physical and emotional health is profound and well-documented. Physical activities such as yoga and regular exercise not only strengthen the body but also have a direct impact on emotional resilience. Yoga, for example, combines physical postures with breathwork and meditation, promoting relaxation and stress management. Regular exercise releases endorphins, chemicals in your brain that act as natural painkillers and mood elevators. These activities improve not only physical fitness but also contribute to a more resilient emotional state by reducing symptoms of anxiety and depression, enhancing self-esteem, and improving sleep.

Success stories abound in regards to resilience training. Consider the case of Alex, a young professional who struggled with severe anxiety due to the high demands of his tech job. By incorporating regular yoga sessions into his routine and engaging in resilience training exercises, Alex was able to significantly reduce his anxiety. He found that he could handle stressful situations at work with more calmness and clarity. His success story is not unique; many have found that through resilience training, they are not only able to face challenges more effectively but also experience greater overall well-being.

These exercises like practicing visualization, scenario planning, resilience drills, and by maintaining a routine that includes physical activities like yoga will help you enhance your ability to go through life's challenges with greater ease and confidence. As you continue to train and build your *emotional muscle,* you'll find yourself not only bouncing back faster from setbacks but also moving forward with an increased capacity for handling whatever life throws your way.

THE POWER OF POSITIVE AFFIRMATIONS IN BUILDING RESILIENCE

In our minds, the words we tell ourselves plant either positive or negative thoughts in it. This internal dialogue, often unnoticed, shapes our reality by influencing our beliefs about ourselves and our capabilities. It's here that the power of positive affirmations can be transformative, especially when building resilience against life's adversities. *Positive affirmations* are deliberate, empowering statements used to challenge and undermine negative thoughts, and when practiced consistently, they reinforce self-esteem and resilience, turning negative thoughts in our mind into positive ones for growth.

The key to using affirmations effectively lies in their construction and relevance to your personal experiences and aspirations. To construct affirmations that deeply resonate to you, start by identifying areas in your life where you feel vulnerable or face self-doubt. For example, if you frequently feel inadequate in your professional abilities, an affirmation like "I am competent and skilled in my work" can be a robust counter to this specific insecurity. Similarly, if anxiety in social situations is a challenge, an affirmation such as "I am calm and articulate in social settings" might be beneficial. The affirmation should always be *positive*, stated in the *present tense*, and expressed *as a fact.* This helps your mind to accept it as your current reality, not a future possibility.

Incorporating these affirmations into your daily routine will significantly amplify their impact in your life. One effective method is to integrate them into your morning routine. Early in the day, our minds are like blank slates and introducing positive affirmations can set a constructive tone for the hours ahead. You might consider saying your affirmations aloud in front of a mirror, a practice that enhances the connection between your spoken words and self-image. Alternatively, meditation sessions offer a quiet moment to mentally or softly repeat your affirmations, allowing them to sink deeper into your consciousness. By making affirmations a regular practice, just as brushing your teeth or having breakfast, they become embedded into your daily life, steadily working to shift your internal narrative from critical or doubtful to empowering and affirmative.

Studies in the field of neuroplasticity have shown that consistent positive self-talk can rewire the brain's pathways, leading to changes in how we think and feel. Moreover, testimonials from individuals who have embraced this practice often speak of profound shifts in their confidence and outlook on life. For example, there was a young entrepreneur who battled with imposter syndrome, a common plight where one doubts their achievements and harbors a persistent fear of being exposed as a "fraud." By adhering to a daily regimen of affirmations focused on her capabilities and successes, she was able to dismantle these fears and significantly boost her confidence, leading to better decision-making and increased opportunities in her business ventures.

However, it's important to note that the power of affirmations extends beyond combating negative thoughts; they also play a crucial role in reinforcing the lessons learned from past experiences. Each time you affirm your strength, wisdom, or courage, you are not only reminding yourself of your ability to overcome future challenges but also acknowledging and validating your past struggles. This acknowledgment acts as a bridge between past experiences and future endeavors, fortifying your psychological resilience.

As you continue to nurture this practice, you may find that what once felt like insurmountable challenges now seem like opportunities for growth and self-discovery.

ROLE OF MINDFULNESS IN RESILIENCE

Mindfulness, a term that has echoed through in modern therapy and personal development practices, represents a mental state of awareness, focus, and openness that helps individuals anchor themselves firmly in the present moment. It involves an intentional act of paying attention to thoughts, emotions, and sensations without judgment. This practice is particularly relevant to building resilience as it provides a tool to go through life's stressors by fostering a deep, sustainable form of mental clarity and emotional stability.

When you practice mindfulness, you cultivate a core skill set that allows you to endure and bounce back from the mental and emotional challenges of everyday life. For instance, consider the moments when stress begins to creep in, whether from looming deadlines or personal conflicts. By engaging in mindfulness, you can observe these stressors without immediately reacting to them. This pause is crucial—it provides the space to choose how to respond to challenges more thoughtfully and less impulsively, which is the cornerstone of resilience.

To integrate mindfulness into your daily life, begin with simple exercises that can be practiced anywhere at any time. One foundational practice is mindful breathing, where you focus solely on your breath, observing each inhalation and exhalation without attempting to change or regulate it. This exercise anchors your mind in the present moment and can be a quick and effective method to regain your emotional equilibrium when you start to feel the stirrings of stress or anxiety.

Another practical exercise is the body scan, which involves mentally scanning your body for areas of tension and consciously relaxing these areas. Start from the top of your head and move slowly down to your toes. By progressively relaxing each part of your body, you not only release physical tension but also learn to identify how your emotions affect your body, which can be particularly enlightening during moments of stress or discomfort.

The benefits of mindfulness extend well beyond simple stress management. Regular practice can fundamentally decrease emotional reactivity. Instead of being tossed about by the waves of your emotions, mindfulness offers you a surfboard to ride them more gracefully. It helps in recognizing the early signs of emotional distress and provides you with the tools to calm yourself down before your feelings become overwhelming. This enhanced mood stability is crucial for maintaining long-term mental health and fostering resilience.

Furthermore, mindfulness has been shown to improve overall emotional and mental well-being. It encourages a positive outlook on life, increases patience and tolerance, and enhances cognitive function. These benefits are not just subjective. Neuroscience research has provided concrete evidence supporting the efficacy of mindfulness. Studies using brain imaging technology have shown that mindfulness meditation can lead to changes in the brain areas related to attention, emotion regulation, and self-awareness. Regular practitioners of mindfulness show increased activity in the prefrontal cortex, the part of the brain associated with positive emotion and engaged living, which can help combat the neural mechanisms that produce anxiety and depression.

Incorporating mindfulness into your routine requires consistency, but the investment of time and effort is well rewarded. As you become more adept at noticing your thoughts and feelings without judgment, you'll likely find yourself responding to life's challenges with increased calm and resilience. Whether it's through mindful breathing during a hectic day or a full body scan during a quiet evening, mindfulness offers a powerful set of tools for enhancing your emotional resilience and overall well-being. By fostering a deep, sustained connection to the present moment, mindfulness empowers you to face life's stressors with steadiness and clarity.

LEARNING FROM PAST EMOTIONAL CHALLENGES

Reflecting on past emotional challenges is not merely about revisiting painful memories; it's a proactive approach to distill wisdom from experiences and fortify your emotional resilience. When you deliberately examine past hardships, you uncover patterns, strengths, and areas needing improvement, turning past adversities into lessons that propel personal growth and emotional fortitude. This process of reflective learning is about extracting valuable insights from the raw experiences of your life.

To engage in reflective learning, start by recalling a specific emotional challenge you faced. Perhaps it was a job loss, a difficult breakup, or a period of intense anxiety. Describe the situation in detail, including what you felt and how you responded. Then, ask yourself structured questions that help you analyze the scenario critically. What triggered your emotional response? What coping strategies did you use, and how effective were they? What could you have done differently? By answering these questions, you not only gain clarity about how you manage difficulties but also identify strategies that could be improved or strengthened for future challenges.

A *workbook-style template* can be an invaluable tool in this reflective process. It can guide you through a series of prompts designed to help you methodically break down your experiences and extract actionable insights. For instance, the template might prompt you to list out the emotions you felt during the challenge, describe the thoughts that accompanied these emotions, and note the immediate and long-term actions you took in response. This structured approach ensures that no aspect of the experience is overlooked and that you derive the maximum learning from each situation.

Acceptance plays a pivotal role in learning from past challenges. It involves acknowledging and coming to terms with the outcomes of your experiences, regardless of whether they were positive or negative. This doesn't mean resigning yourself to your fate but rather embracing your past with a sense of peace, understanding that every experience has contributed to your growth. Acceptance frees you from the burden of past regrets and empowers you to move forward with confidence and openness to new experiences. It allows you to take the lessons learned and apply them constructively as you face new challenges, enhancing both your resilience and your ability to navigate life's ups and downs.

Inspirational recovery stories serve as powerful reminders of the human capacity to overcome adversity and emerge stronger. Consider Maya, who endured a severe illness that left her isolated and depressed. Through her recovery, she learned the importance of self-care and seeking support, which not only helped her heal but also inspired her to become a mental health advocate. Another example is John, who faced significant financial difficulties after a business failure. The experience taught him valuable lessons about risk management, resilience, and the importance of maintaining a work-life balance. These stories not only offer hope and motivation but also illustrate the practical applications of the lessons learned from facing and overcoming emotional challenges.

Reflecting on and learning from past emotional challenges is more than a process; it's a journey of self-discovery that strengthens your resilience and prepares you for future adversities. By embracing this practice, you will equip yourself with a deeper understanding of your emotional dynamics, enhance your coping strategies, and foster a robustness that will permeate all areas of your life. As you move forward, let the lessons learned illuminate your path, guiding you with wisdom gleaned from the challenges you've overcome.

As we conclude this exploration of learning from past emotional challenges, remember that each difficulty you encounter is an opportunity to grow stronger and wiser. As we transition into the next chapter, keep in mind the strength you've garnered from past experiences and the proactive steps you can take to fortify your resilience even further.

STRATEGIES FOR SELF-PROTECTION

*D*ealing with the complexities of everyday interactions, whether in personal or professional settings, demands a toolkit equipped not just with good intentions, but with effective communication strategies. Imagine you're at a street market, surrounded by vendors. Each vendor uses a different approach to grab your attention; some shout loudly, some bargain gently, while others might calmly explain the value of their goods. Similarly, how we communicate our needs and feelings in relationships can significantly impact the outcomes we experience, making the mastery of *assertive communication* a crucial skill in your self-protection arsenal.

ASSERTIVE COMMUNICATION: EXPRESSING YOUR NEEDS CLEARLY

Defining Assertive Communication

Assertiveness is a communication style rooted in respect—for yourself and others. *It is the balanced middle ground between aggression and passivity.* When you communicate assertively, you express your thoughts, feelings, and needs openly and straightforwardly, without undermining the rights and feelings of others. It's about being honest and direct while maintaining a calm and positive demeanor. This style of communication is fundamental not only to your self-esteem and mental health but also to building and maintaining healthy relationships.

Differentiating Between Assertive and Aggressive Communication

To distinguish assertiveness from aggression, consider their core intentions and impacts. Aggressive communication often involves making demands, using a loud tone, and sometimes even belittling others to get one's way, which can lead to resentment and damage relationships. On the other hand, assertive communication respects your rights and those of others, fostering understanding and collaboration. For example, while an aggressive communicator might say, "You never listen to me, you need to change your attitude!", an assertive communicator would say, "I feel frustrated when I'm not heard because my opinions also matter. Can we discuss this further?"

Teaching the Components of Assertive Communication

Mastering assertive communication involves several key components:

- **"I" Statements**: These are expressions that focus on the speaker's feelings rather than blaming or criticizing the listener. For instance, saying "I feel overwhelmed when I have to finish projects at the last minute" instead of "You always dump things on me at the last minute."

- **Clear Language**: Being assertive means being clear and specific about what you want, think, or feel. Ambiguity can lead to misunderstandings. Instead of saying "I wish people would respect my time," specify, "I prefer if we start our meetings on time as it helps me manage my schedule better."
- **Non-verbal Cues**: Your body language, facial expressions, and eye contact should align with your words. Maintaining eye contact shows confidence and sincerity, while an open stance can make you appear more approachable and engaged.

Role-playing Scenarios

Engaging in role-playing can significantly enhance your assertive communication skills by providing a safe environment to practice and receive feedback. Consider these scenarios:

- **At Work**: You are assigned a last-minute task that would require you to stay late. Practice how you would assertively communicate your inability to stay late due to prior commitments and suggest an alternative deadline.
- **In Family Settings**: A family member often criticizes your life choices. Role-play how you would use "I"

statements to express how this makes you feel and request a more supportive approach.

- **In Social Circles**: A friend constantly cancels plans last-minute, leaving you frustrated. Role-play an assertive conversation where you express your feelings and discuss how you can make plans more reliably in the future.

Through these exercises, you'll not only refine your verbal and non-verbal assertive communication skills but also build confidence in handling various interpersonal situations assertively. This confidence is key to protecting your emotional health and ensuring your interactions are respectful and productive.

THE IMPORTANCE OF SAYING NO: PRACTICAL EXERCISES

Learning to say 'no' is an invaluable aspect of self-protection and preserving your personal boundaries. It's about respecting your own time, energy, and preferences. However, many of us struggle with this simple word due to deep-seated fears of disappointing others or disrupting harmony. The discomfort associated with saying 'no' often stems from a worry about how it will be received—will it hurt someone's feelings, or will it be viewed as selfish? Overcoming these emotional barriers is not just liberative; it's essential for maintaining your emotional health and ensuring that your relationships are genuinely reciprocal.

One common emotional barrier is the *guilt* associated with saying 'no.' This guilt can be paralyzing, making it easier sometimes to agree against your better judgment. To combat this, start by recognizing that saying 'no' does not make you a bad or selfish person. *It simply means you are making a choice that prioritizes your well-being.* It's helpful to remind yourself that by saying 'no,' you are not denying a request out of spite but rather making a decision based on your current capabilities and needs.

To further ease the guilt, consider the consequences of always saying 'yes.' Often, this leads to overcommitment, stress, and even resentment—emotions that are far more damaging to relationships than a respectful 'no.' Reflect on times when you've felt overwhelmed due to your inability to decline requests. How did it affect your mood and interactions with others? This reflection can reinforce the importance and necessity of *saying 'no' as a form of self-care.*

Practicing saying 'no' can be daunting, so it's beneficial to start small. Begin with low-stakes situations where the repercussions of declining are minimal. For example, if a colleague asks if you have time to chat while you are busy, practice saying, "I'm in the middle of something right now, can we talk later?" Gradually, as your comfort with declining requests grows, you can apply this practice to more significant or emotionally charged requests, such as turning down an invitation to a social event when you need time for yourself.

To make this process more concrete, here are step-by-step exercises to practice saying 'no':

1. **Identify Opportunities to Say No**: Start by recognizing situations daily where you could say 'no,' but typically don't. These could be as simple as not accepting an unwanted phone call to more complex scenarios like declining extra responsibilities at work.

2. **Prepare Your Response**: Before you find yourself in a situation where you need to say 'no,' prepare your response. Decide on the language that feels comfortable and practice saying it out loud. You might say, "Thank you for considering me, but I won't be able to commit to that this week," or "I appreciate your invitation, but I have other plans."

3. **Follow Through with Confidence**: When the moment comes, deliver your response calmly and confidently. Maintain a polite but firm tone, and avoid over-explaining or making excuses, as this can invite negotiation.

4. **Reflect on the Experience**: Afterward, take some time to reflect on the experience. How did it feel to say no? What was the reaction? How did you handle it? This reflection will prepare you for future situations and help build your confidence.

Sharing success stories where saying no has led to positive outcomes can also be incredibly empowering. For instance, consider the story of a project manager who often felt pressured to take on more projects than she could handle. After learning to say 'no,' she not only managed her workload more effectively but also noticed an improvement in her team's respect for her time and her overall job satisfaction. Another example is from a young writer who frequently helped friends with their projects. When she started saying 'no,' she found more time to focus on her own work, leading to a significant breakthrough in her career.

These stories highlight that while the act of saying 'no' might be difficult initially, the benefits it brings—such as increased self-respect, better time management, and improved personal relationships—are profound and far-reaching. As you continue to practice and integrate this vital skill into your life, you'll find that saying 'no' not only protects your time and energy but also opens up space for choices and commitments that are truly meaningful to you.

DETOXIFYING YOUR ENVIRONMENT: PRACTICAL STEPS

In our daily lives, the environments we inhabit—both physical and virtual—can significantly influence our emotional health and overall well-being. Just as a gardener must regularly weed their garden to prevent the overgrowth of unwanted plants, you must also tend to the various environments you occupy, removing toxic elements to foster a healthier, more nourishing atmosphere. This process, often referred to as *detoxification*, isn't just about removing negatives but also about enhancing your space with positive influences that encourage growth and promote well-being.

The first step in this process is to identify the sources of toxicity in your environment. This might include relationships that drain your emotional energy, cluttered living spaces that cause stress and anxiety, or digital interactions that provoke negativity or distract you from more meaningful activities. For instance, consider the friend who consistently shares pessimistic views that dampen your mood, or the clutter in your home office that makes you feel overwhelmed and stressed. On the digital front, excessive consumption of news or social media that stirs up feelings of inadequacy or anger can also be significant sources of environmental toxicity. By taking stock of these factors, you can begin to map out what elements need to be addressed to create a more positive environment.

Once you've identified these toxic elements, the next step is to create a structured plan to reduce or remove them from your life. This might involve having difficult conversations with people whose presence in your life is more harmful than beneficial, organizing and decluttering your physical spaces to create a more serene environment, or setting limits on your digital engagement to reduce exposure to negative content. For example, you might decide to spend only a specific amount of time per day on social media or choose to engage only with content that uplifts and informs rather than distresses. Similarly, in your physical spaces, techniques like the *KonMari* method, which focuses on keeping only those items that 'spark joy,' can be an effective way to declutter and detoxify your living or working environments.

Replacing toxic elements with positive influences is crucial to ensuring the long-term health and positivity of your environment. This involves fostering relationships that are supportive and uplifting, curating physical and digital spaces that inspire and comfort, and engaging in activities that enhance your sense of well-being. Cultivate friendships with individuals who encourage and empower you, and invest time in these relationships. In your physical environment, consider introducing elements that reduce stress, such as plants, which have been shown to lower workplace stress and enhance productivity, or setting up a dedicated nook for relaxation and meditation. Digitally, curate your feeds to include inspirational and educational content, and follow accounts that contribute positively to your mental health and personal growth.

Regular assessment and adjustment of your environment are essential to maintaining its health and relevance to your needs. This ongoing process involves periodically reevaluating the elements of your environment to ensure they still contribute positively to your life. Change is constant, and what may have been a positive influence at one point can become less so over time. Regularly asking yourself whether certain relationships, habits, or items still serve your well-being is key. This might mean reassessing the boundaries you've set with others, revisiting your digital consumption habits, or rearranging your living space to reflect changes in your lifestyle or personal goals. By staying active and responsive to these needs, you ensure that your environment remains a supportive backdrop to your life's evolving story.

Through these steps, detoxifying your environment becomes a dynamic and proactive process that not only removes the negative influences in your life but also enhances your surroundings with positive energy and support. This balanced approach not only improves your immediate surroundings but also contributes to a sustained sense of well-being, allowing you to thrive in environments that are not just free of toxicity but also rich in nurturing and supportive energies.

NURTURING SELF-CARE PRACTICES TO GUARD AGAINST TOXICITY

Self-care is often portrayed as a luxury, but in reality, it's a fundamental practice crucial for maintaining both mental and physical health. It acts as a protective barrier, shielding you from the detrimental effects of stress and toxicity that life invariably throws your way. Think of self-care as the armor you wear into battle; it's essential for your survival and effectiveness. By engaging in self-care, you're not just indulging in momentary pleasures—you're systematically reinforcing your health, fortifying your resilience, and ensuring your long-term well-being.

Self-care covers a wide range of practices that cater to various needs and preferences. These can range from physical activities like yoga and running, which not only improve physical health but also relieve stress, to hobbies such as painting or gardening that provide a creative outlet and mental relaxation. Social interactions are also a critical component of self-care; connecting with friends or participating in community activities can offer emotional support and alleviate feelings of loneliness or isolation. Additionally, relaxation techniques such as meditation, deep breathing exercises, or even a simple routine of reading before bed can significantly reduce anxiety and foster a calm mind.

Developing a personal self-care plan is a proactive step towards enhancing your quality of life. This plan should reflect your unique circumstances, including your lifestyle, work schedule, and personal preferences. Start by assessing your current self-care practices—what are you doing now for your well-being? Identify areas that might be lacking; perhaps you're neglecting physical exercise or social interactions. Then, set realistic goals to integrate more of these activities into your routine. Remember, the effectiveness of self-care lies in its regular practice, so it's crucial to choose activities that you enjoy and can sustain over the long term.

For instance, if you find it hard to make time for exercise, consider activities that can be integrated into your daily routine, such as biking to work or taking a walking meeting instead of sitting in a conference room. If your schedule is erratic, short meditation sessions of 5-10 minutes might be more feasible than longer sessions. The key is to tailor your self-care activities to fit your life realistically, ensuring that they enhance rather than become a burden.

Consistent engagement in self-care practices plays a pivotal role in building emotional resilience. This resilience acts like a buffer, helping you to manage stress more effectively and maintain equilibrium in the face of life's challenges. Regular self-care not only helps to prevent the onset of stress-related illness but also enhances your ability to cope with existing health conditions. It strengthens your emotional foundations, making you less vulnerable to external pressures and improving your overall ability to perform and enjoy life.

Incorporating self-care into your daily routine might require some adjustments initially, but the benefits it brings are profound as it empowers you to take control of your health and well-being, actively preventing the toxic influences of stress and negativity from taking root. You'll notice significant improvements as you continue to explore and implement these practices, not only in your physical and emotional health but also in your relationships and productivity. You're setting the stage for a fuller, more satisfying life by taking care of yourself.

As we conclude this chapter on self-care, remember that the practices you choose can serve as your personal sanctuary—spaces and activities where you can recharge and refocus. By committing to regular self-care, you are not only protecting yourself from toxicity but also enhancing your resilience, ensuring you are better equipped to handle whatever challenges come your way.

The next chapter will build on the foundation we've established here, exploring advanced strategies for managing emotional triggers and maintaining mental health in the face of ongoing stressors. As you continue to deepen your commitment to self-care, these upcoming discussions will offer further insights and tools to support your journey toward sustained emotional well-being.

OVERCOMING EMOTIONAL OVERWHELM

*I*magine standing in the center of a very busy city intersection, the noise of the crowd and the ceaseless traffic creating a cacophony that surrounds you. Feeling overwhelmed in this setting feels almost inevitable. Now, consider this scenario as a metaphor for the social settings we navigate daily, where the buzz of conversation, the flurry of activity, and the pressure to perform can sometimes lead to profound anxiety. This chapter is dedicated to equipping you with strategies to manage and overcome the emotional overwhelm that can arise in social environments, enhancing your ability to thrive in these settings.

Techniques for Managing Anxiety in Social Settings

Identify Anxiety Triggers in Social Environments

The first step in managing social anxiety effectively is recognizing what triggers your anxiety in these settings. Triggers can vary widely among individuals; for some, large groups might provoke anxiety, while for others, public speaking or informal social gatherings could be the stressors. By identifying these triggers, you can begin to understand and address the root causes of your discomfort. For instance, if speaking in public is a trigger, is it the fear of judgment or perhaps a past embarrassing moment that fuels this anxiety? Or, if large groups make you uneasy, could it be the chaotic energy or the fear of being unnoticed or overlooked that affects you? Understanding these triggers is crucial as it forms the basis for applying effective management strategies.

Introduce Grounding Techniques

Grounding techniques are invaluable tools for managing anxiety symptoms, especially in settings where you might feel overwhelmed. These techniques help divert your focus from the anxiety-inducing stimulus and bring your attention back to the present moment, reducing the intensity of your anxiety. One effective grounding technique is *focused breathing*, where you concentrate solely on your respiration, taking slow, deep breaths to calm your nervous system. Another technique involves sensory awareness—paying close attention to the physical sensations of the objects around you, like the feel of the chair you're sitting on or the texture of the glass you're holding. These practices can be discreetly used in social settings, offering a quick and effective way to manage your anxiety without drawing attention to yourself.

Role-Play Common Social Situations

Role-playing can be a powerful method to prepare for and practice handling anxiety-inducing social situations. By simulating the scenarios that trigger your anxiety, you can experiment with different ways of responding, building your confidence and ability to cope. For example, if interacting at networking events is challenging, role-play these interactions with a friend or in a therapy setting. Practice introducing yourself, asking engaging questions, and even excusing yourself from the conversation. Through role-play, you can develop a repertoire of responses that make you feel more secure and self-assured, reducing the likelihood of anxiety taking over in real situations.

Encourage Gradual Exposure

Gradual exposure involves slowly and systematically exposing yourself to the situations that trigger your anxiety, in a controlled and planned manner. The idea is to desensitize yourself to the anxiety triggers by gradually increasing your exposure to them, which over time, can significantly reduce your anxiety response. For example, if speaking in front of a group is a trigger, you might start by speaking to a small, familiar group, and incrementally increase the size of the audience as your comfort level improves. This method not only helps in reducing sensitivity to the triggers but also empowers you with the confidence that you can manage and overcome the anxiety associated with social interactions.

Through these techniques—identifying triggers, using grounding methods, role-playing, and gradual exposure—you can move through social settings with greater ease and confidence. Each strategy offers a tool to manage the symptoms of anxiety effectively, ensuring that you are equipped to face rather than fear social interactions. As you incorporate these techniques into your daily routines, you'll find that the overwhelming noise of the metaphorical city intersection we mentioned before, becomes more like a background hum, allowing you to engage with your social environment proactively and positively.

HANDLING EMOTIONAL OVERWHELM AT WORK

In your fast-paced workplace, where deadlines loom large and responsibilities mount, managing stress and maintaining emotional equilibrium are not just beneficial; they are necessary for sustained productivity and personal well-being. One effective strategy to mitigate stress is the implementation of *structured breaks* throughout your workday. These are not merely pauses in your schedule but strategic timeouts that allow your mind to reset and your emotions to stabilize. By stepping away from your desk at regular intervals—perhaps every 90 minutes or so—you can significantly reduce feelings of overwhelm and refresh your focus. Think of these breaks as pressing a brief 'pause' on your workday, providing a moment to breathe deeply, stretch, or take a quick walk outside. The key is consistency and mindfulness during these breaks; use this time to genuinely disengage from work-related thoughts, immersing yourself in a different activity that rejuvenates your spirit and sharpens your focus for the tasks ahead.

Equally important in managing workplace stress is mastering the art of prioritization and delegation. In many cases, overwhelm stems not just from the volume of work but also from a disorganized approach to handling it. Start by evaluating your tasks based on urgency and importance. Tools like the *Eisenhower Box*, a decision-making tool that helps prioritizing tasks by categorizing them into four categories: urgent and important, important, but not urgent, urgent, neither urgent nor important, can be invaluable here, helping you decide whether tasks need to be done immediately, scheduled for later, delegated, or not done at all. Delegation, while often underused, is a critical skill that involves recognizing tasks that others can handle and communicating these tasks effectively. It's about trusting your team with responsibilities that free you up to focus on work only you can perform. Remember, delegation is not a sign of weakness, but a strategic decision that leverages the strengths of your team for optimal outcomes.

Developing an *emotional emergency plan* is another proactive measure to handle moments of acute stress at work. This plan involves identifying a private space where you can retreat to regain composure—perhaps a rarely used conference room or even a nearby park. Equip this space with items that help soothe you, such as a book, calming music, or a stress-relief gadget. Additionally, outline techniques that help you regain calm, such as deep breathing exercises or visualization. Knowing who in your workplace can offer support—whether a sympathetic colleague or a mentor—can also be part of this emergency plan. Having such a plan in place ensures that when overwhelming feelings strike, you're not at a loss but have a clear path to stabilization.

Finally, *establishing and maintaining professional boundaries* is crucial for protecting your emotional health. These boundaries help define what you are willing to tolerate and how you expect to be treated by colleagues and supervisors. Clear boundaries can prevent burnout by ensuring you do not overextend yourself or get caught in roles that drain your energy without offering fulfillment or advancement. Communicate your boundaries clearly—for instance, if late-night emails are encroaching on your personal time, specify that you will respond during work hours. Be firm and consistent, as this sets a precedent for how you are willing to manage your work-life balance. Remember, setting boundaries is not about creating barriers but about fostering a work environment where you can thrive without compromising your well-being.

By integrating these strategies—taking structured breaks, prioritizing and delegating tasks, establishing an emotional emergency plan, and setting professional boundaries—you create a sustainable approach to managing work-related stress. These practices not only enhance your productivity and professional relationships but also safeguard your mental health, allowing you to go through the challenges of your career with resilience and confidence.

TOOLS FOR CALMING ANGER QUICKLY

In the heat of an emotional moment, anger can feel like a simmering pot ready to boil over. Sometimes, it might catch you off guard, escalating quickly and affecting your actions and responses. Managing this intense emotion requires effective techniques that can swiftly bring your temper under control, ensuring that your reactions remain measured and appropriate. One particularly effective method is the *"STOP" technique* —an acronym that stands for "Stop, Take a breath, Observe, and Proceed." This technique serves as a mental pause button, providing a straightforward way to halt escalating emotions and reflect before responding. When you feel anger bubbling up, simply stop what you're doing. This immediate pause helps prevent your emotions from taking the wheel. Next, take a deep breath to calm your physiological responses; deep breathing helps reduce the physical symptoms of anger, such as a racing heart or tensed muscles. After breathing, take a moment to observe the situation. What triggered your anger? Is it a misunderstanding, or perhaps a deep-seated issue that needs addressing? This reflection can provide clarity and prevent an impulsive reaction. Finally, proceed with your response. This might involve expressing your feelings in a calm and collected manner, or choosing to walk away if the situation requires cooling off.

Physical activity is another powerful tool for managing anger. Engaging in physical activities, such as brisk walking, jogging, or any form of exercise, can significantly help dissipate the energy and tension that accompany anger. Physical movements trigger the release of endorphins, often known as feel-good hormones, which can elevate your mood and reduce feelings of anger. For a quick and immediate release, try squeezing a stress ball or clenching and relaxing your fists. This physical exertion provides an outlet for your energy and helps lessen the emotional intensity you're experiencing. Over time, regular physical activity not only helps in managing moments of anger but also contributes to a generally calmer and more stable emotional state.

Cognitive reframing is a vital skill in transforming the way you perceive and react to potential anger triggers. This technique involves altering your perspective on a situation to view it in a more positive or realistic light. For instance, if you're angry over a coworker's remark, reframe your thoughts from "They're always out to get me" to "Perhaps they didn't realize how their words might affect me." This shift in perspective can reduce the intensity of your anger and open up a pathway for constructive dialogue and resolution. Cognitive reframing helps by changing your thought patterns from automatically negative to more balanced and considered, thus reducing the likelihood of anger taking control.

Implementing *timeout strategies* is crucial when dealing with anger, especially in situations where emotions continue to escalate despite initial management efforts. A timeout involves stepping away from the situation to prevent your anger from leading to regrettable actions. This can be as simple as excusing yourself to take a walk or retreating to a quiet space where you can gather your thoughts. During this time, engage in introspection or relaxation techniques to calm down fully. The key is to give yourself enough space and time to cool down before revisiting the issue, ensuring that when you do, you're in a better state of mind to handle the situation constructively.

By incorporating these tools into your emotional toolkit, you equip yourself with effective strategies for managing anger quickly and efficiently. Whether it's through the STOP technique, engaging in physical activity, cognitive reframing, or taking timeouts, these methods provide practical ways to maintain your composure and ensure that your responses are thoughtful and measured. As you continue to practice these techniques, you'll find that you're not only better at controlling your anger but also more adept at navigating the challenges of daily interactions without losing your temper.

OVERCOMING FEAR OF REJECTION

The fear of rejection can often feel like a shadow following closely behind your every social interaction, whispering doubts and conjuring scenarios of disappointment and judgment. It's a universal experience, rooted deeply in our fundamental need for acceptance and belonging. Understanding where this fear originates is crucial to managing it effectively. Common sources include past experiences where rejection was painful or humiliating, often during formative years. These experiences can leave a lasting imprint, leading you to anticipate and fear similar outcomes in your current life. Additionally, low self-esteem can exacerbate this fear, as you might feel inherently unworthy of acceptance, making the prospect of rejection even more daunting.

Addressing these roots involves a process of introspection and reevaluation of past incidents that contributed to this deep-seated fear. Reflecting on these experiences and understanding their impact on your perception of rejection can help you begin to dissociate these past events from your current reality. It's helpful to acknowledge that past rejections were not solely about your worth but also involved circumstances and other individuals' preferences and personal issues. This understanding can gradually reduce the intensity of the fear.

Building resilience against the fear of rejection involves exposing yourself to it in small, controlled increments—a technique known as graduated exposure. You might start by expressing an unpopular opinion in a safe environment or asking for small favors that carry a risk of refusal. These exercises are designed to gradually desensitize your emotional response to rejection, making it more manageable. Each exposure provides an opportunity to handle rejection in real-time, reinforcing your ability to cope with it effectively. Over time, these experiences build a kind of emotional muscle memory, making you less sensitive to rejection and more confident in your interactions.

In parallel, practicing self-affirmations can also bolster your self-esteem significantly and reduce the negative self-talk that often accompanies the fear of rejection. Positive affirmations focus on your *strengths* and *values*, reinforcing your self-worth independently of others' approval. Phrases like "I am valued and respected regardless of others' opinions" or "I am competent and confident in my abilities" can be powerful antidotes to the internal critic that magnifies the fear of rejection. Integrate these affirmations into your daily routine, perhaps by saying them aloud every morning or writing them in a journal. Over time, these positive affirmations can reshape your internal narrative, making you more resilient against the fear of rejection.

Another effective strategy is to change your perspective on rejection. Instead of viewing it as a personal failure or a reflection of your worth, try to see it as a normal part of life—an experience that everyone goes through and that can lead to growth and better opportunities. This cognitive reframing involves actively challenging your existing beliefs about rejection. When faced with rejection, instead of defaulting to self-criticism, ask yourself what you can learn from the experience. Perhaps it revealed areas where you could improve, or maybe it steered you away from a path not meant for you. By viewing rejection as a stepping stone rather than a setback, you reduce its emotional sting and can approach future situations with more confidence and less fear.

These strategies—understanding the origins of your fear, building resilience through exposure, reinforcing your self-esteem with affirmations, and reframing your perspective on rejection—equip you with a robust toolkit to manage and overcome the fear of rejection. As you implement these practices, you'll find that your fear of rejection will continue to diminish and be replaced by a growing confidence and a more secure sense of self-worth that empowers you to engage more openly and authentically in all areas of your life.

STRATEGIES TO COPE WITH JEALOUSY

Jealousy, often viewed as a complex and misunderstood emotion, can be a significant source of distress in personal relationships and individual well-being. It typically arises when we perceive a threat to something we value highly, particularly our relationships, but its roots can be deeply embedded in personal insecurities, past experiences, or unmet emotional needs. Understanding the basis of jealousy is crucial in addressing its manifestations healthily and constructively.

To begin with, exploring the root causes of your jealousy is an essential step. It could be triggered by a variety of factors, from insecurity about one's worth or abilities to traumatic past relationships where trust was breached. For instance, if you often find yourself feeling jealous in your current relationship, consider whether these feelings stem from past betrayals that have left you wary, or perhaps from an internal narrative that you are not enough. Identifying these underlying factors allows you to address them directly, rather than allowing jealousy to dictate your reactions and relationships.

Promoting self-awareness and encouraging personal reflection are vital in this process. Engaging in self-reflection exercises can help you explore and understand your feelings of jealousy more deeply. Consider maintaining a journal where you record instances when you feel jealous, noting what triggered the feeling, how you reacted, and what thoughts accompanied these emotions. Over time, patterns may emerge that highlight specific insecurities or fears fueling your jealousy. This practice not only aids in self-discovery but also fosters greater emotional intelligence, allowing you to manage your reactions more effectively.

There are various techniques that can help regulate these feelings associated with jealousy. *Mindfulness meditation* is a powerful tool, as it encourages you to remain present and aware without judgment. Through mindfulness, you can observe your feelings of jealousy without attaching to them or allowing them to escalate. This can help decrease their intensity and frequency. Another useful technique is *thought-stopping*, which involves consciously interrupting negative thought cycles that fuel jealous feelings. When you find yourself dwelling on thoughts that feed your jealousy, actively say 'stop' in your mind, or even aloud, to disrupt the thought pattern and redirect your focus to more positive or neutral thoughts.

Another crucial aspect of dealing with jealousy involves *communication and transparency* in your relationships. Expressing your feelings openly and honestly can prevent misunderstandings and build trust. When discussing your feelings of jealousy, focus on expressing your emotions *without blaming or accusing the other person*. For example, instead of saying, "You made me jealous by talking to them," try saying, "I felt jealous when I saw you talking to them, and I realize it's something I need to work on." This approach invites dialogue and support, rather than conflict. Additionally, seeking reassurance within your relationships should be done in a way that promotes mutual understanding and trust, without fostering dependency or limiting the other person's freedom.

By understanding the roots of your jealousy, engaging in self-reflection, practicing emotional regulation techniques, and fostering open communication, you can manage jealousy in a way that supports your emotional health and strengthens your relationships. These strategies not only help in alleviating the immediate discomfort caused by jealousy but also contribute to a broader understanding of your emotional responses and how to navigate them effectively.

In this chapter, we've explored various strategies not just for coping with jealousy, but also for addressing anxiety, overwhelm, anger, and rejection. These emotions, if not managed properly, can significantly impact your quality of life and relationships. The tools and insights provided here aim to empower you to face these challenges with confidence and resilience, enhancing your emotional well-being and interpersonal connections.

HEALING FROM EMOTIONAL TRAUMA

*I*magine you're walking through your old neighborhood, and with each step, unexpected sounds trigger vivid memories—some comforting and some unsettling. This scenario shows you how past traumas can linger in your emotional and psychological well-being, influencing your daily life long after the events have passed. Traumas are like shadows that stretch far beyond their origins and color our perceptions and reactions in ways we might not fully understand. In this chapter, we'll explore the enduring impact of trauma on present emotions, helping you to process them and heal from these deep-seated wounds.

UNDERSTANDING THE IMPACT OF PAST TRAUMA ON PRESENT EMOTIONS

Trauma can embed itself in the psyche, acting like a time capsule that bursts open with past pains and fears when triggered by current events. The persistence of trauma is not merely a replay of past events but a continuation of their impact on present emotions and behaviors. For instance, someone who has experienced a betrayal may develop an ongoing fear of trust, affecting their relationships for years to come. This enduring nature of trauma shows that it's not the events themselves but their unresolved emotional aftermath that weaves through the fabric of one's daily life.

Specific situations, people, or environments can serve as triggers, prompting responses that are disproportionately intense compared to the present situation. These triggers are like hidden landmines, unknown until stepped upon, and can result in reactions that may seem excessive or irrational to outsiders. For example, a simple critique from a boss might provoke an extreme anxiety response in someone who was frequently criticized in childhood. The sound of raised voices might evoke distress in someone who grew up in a volatile household. Recognizing these triggers is a critical step toward managing their impact. It involves not only identifying what specifically prompts these reactions but also understanding the underlying emotions tied to them—fear, helplessness, or sadness.

The symptoms of unresolved trauma can manifest in various ways, signaling the need for attention and healing. Common signs include flashbacks, where an individual relives the traumatic event as if it were occurring in the present; persistent fear and anxiety about perceived threats; and avoidance behaviors, where one steers clear of situations or people that remind them of the trauma. Additionally, emotional numbness or detachment can occur, serving as a protective mechanism against the intensity of traumatic memories.

Physiologically, the body's response to trauma can be complex and profound. When faced with traumatic memories or triggers, the body might react with the fight, flight, or freeze responses—instinctual reactions that prepare the body to confront, escape, or become immobile in the face of threats. These responses are mediated by the autonomic nervous system and are essential for survival in dangerous situations. However, when repeatedly activated by trauma triggers, they can lead to chronic stress, manifesting physically as insomnia, muscle tension, fatigue, and other health issues. Understanding these physiological responses is essential for recognizing the signs of trauma in the body and employing strategies to manage them effectively.

Visual Element: The Fight, Flight, or Freeze Response

An infographic detailing the fight, flight, or freeze response can help visualize how the body reacts to trauma. It can illustrate the physiological changes associated with each response, such as increased heart rate (fight), rapid breathing (flight), or a sense of paralysis (freeze). This visual aid underscores the importance of recognizing these responses in oneself and understanding their origins in past trauma.

Recognizing and understanding the persistence of trauma, its triggers, symptoms, and physiological responses, are foundational in the journey toward healing. It allows for a compassionate self-awareness that facilitates the processing and integration of traumatic experiences. As we continue to explore these themes, remember that the goal is not to erase the past but to understand and transform its influence on your present and future life.

THERAPEUTIC APPROACHES TO HEALING FROM EMOTIONAL TRAUMA

When it comes to psychological healing, *Trauma-Focused Cognitive Behavioral Therapy (TF-CBT)* is a prominent approach for those looking to heal the psychological scars left by traumatic experiences. This specialized form of cognitive behavioral therapy is designed to address the complex emotional and psychological needs of trauma survivors. TF-CBT helps individuals reframe and recover from traumatic memories by focusing on the thoughts, feelings, and behaviors that are linked to traumatic experiences. Its core principle is the systematic modification of distorted or unhelpful beliefs related to the trauma. For example, a person who survived a car accident might irrationally believe they are to blame for the incident. Through TF-CBT, they would learn to challenge and reframe this belief, recognizing that it was a circumstance beyond their control, thereby alleviating undue guilt and distress.

The process typically unfolds over several stages, beginning with skills training in areas such as emotional regulation and distress tolerance. This foundation equips individuals with the tools necessary to face and process their traumatic memories in a controlled and therapeutic setting. Subsequent phases involve exposure to trauma memories, narrative development, and cognitive processing, where the therapist helps the individual create a coherent story of the traumatic event, addressing and restructuring harmful thought patterns. In the final stages, the main objectives are to solidify gains, enhance personal safety, and foster future growth. TF-CBT is particularly effective because it not only helps individuals process their trauma but also empowers them with skills that are beneficial for their overall emotional and psychological health.

Another transformative approach to healing from trauma is *Eye Movement Desensitization and Reprocessing (EMDR)*. This innovative therapy is based on the premise that processing traumatic memories can be enhanced by a specific pattern of eye movements. During EMDR sessions, the therapist will guide clients to recall distressing images while simultaneously directing them to perform bilateral stimulation, typically through side-to-side eye movements. This process is believed to facilitate the neural mechanisms involved in the natural processing of traumatic memories, akin to the psychological healing that occurs during Rapid Eye Movement (REM) sleep phases.

EMDR therapy follows a structured format consisting of multiple phases, starting with history taking and treatment planning, followed by preparation, where the therapist ensures that the client has several different ways of handling emotional distress. The core part of the therapy involves identifying and processing distressing memories and negative self-beliefs, replacing them with more adaptive coping mechanisms and beliefs. The effectiveness of EDRM lies in its potential to reduce the emotional pain associated with traumatic memories, often achieving significant therapeutic results in a relatively short period compared to other treatment modalities.

Narrative therapy offers yet another pathway for those healing from trauma. This therapeutic approach is based on the concept that our identities are shaped by the stories we tell about our lives, and that these stories can be rewritten. Narrative therapy helps individuals separate their identity from their traumatic experiences, promoting a view of the self that is not defined by trauma. In practice, this involves identifying the dominant negative narrative that a person has about their life and exploring alternative narratives that highlight personal strengths and achievements. By re-authoring their story, individuals can shift their self-perception from that of a victim to a survivor, or even a thriver, changing how they interact with the world and perceive future possibilities.

The benefits of group therapy for trauma recovery are also profound. Group therapy can provide a supportive environment where you can share your experiences and feelings with others who have faced similar challenges. This setting helps diminish feelings of isolation and fosters a sense of communal healing. The shared experiences within the group can validate your feelings and promote a collective understanding, which is incredibly therapeutic. Participants can learn from each other's coping strategies and offer real-time support, creating a network of empathy and understanding that reinforces personal growth and resilience. The group dynamic can also encourage more reticent individuals to open up and express their feelings, which is a crucial step in the healing process.

Together, these therapeutic approaches offer robust and diverse strategies for healing from trauma. Each method provides unique tools and insights, contributing to a holistic healing journey that addresses the multifaceted nature of trauma and fosters a renewed sense of self and future.

FORGIVENESS: A TOOL FOR HEALING

Forgiveness is often misunderstood when it comes to trauma. It is not about condoning or excusing the harmful actions of others, nor does it require reconciliation with the perpetrator. Instead, forgiveness is a decision, a personal process, a release from the grip of lingering resentment and pain that binds you to past events. It's about finding peace for yourself, letting go of grudges, and moving forward with a lighter heart. This kind of forgiveness is less about altering your past and more about changing your future, allowing you to reclaim your emotional freedom and redirect your energy towards constructive healing. This is easier to achieve when you live a spiritual life - faith in God.

The emotional benefits of embracing forgiveness are profound and multifaceted. Engaging in forgiveness can significantly reduce stress, anxiety, and depression—all common symptoms associated with unresolved trauma. This alleviation of negative emotions is not merely a temporary relief but a lasting change that can dramatically improve your overall quality of life. By forgiving, you shift your focus from what has been done to you towards what you can do for yourself moving forward. This shift is empowering; it places control back into your hands, enabling you to dictate your emotional state and choose responses that align with your desires for health and happiness, rather than reactions dictated by past hurts.

Embarking on the path to forgiveness is not always straightforward; it requires courage, reflection, and often, a structured approach. Here's a step-by-step guide that might help you navigate this challenging but rewarding process:

1. **Acknowledgment of Pain**: Start by acknowledging that you have been hurt. Recognize and validate your feelings, no matter how difficult they might be. Understanding that your pain is real and deserves attention is the first step in the healing process.

2. **Understanding the Context**: Next, try to understand the circumstances or factors that led to the harmful actions. This isn't about justifying what was done, but rather about seeing the situation from a broader perspective. Sometimes, understanding that the person who hurt you was acting out of their own unresolved traumas or limitations can lessen the personal sting of their actions and aid in the forgiveness process.

3. **Choosing to Forgive**: Forgiveness is a choice, and often a difficult one. It involves making a conscious decision to let go of resentment. This step doesn't happen overnight and might require you to revisit your feelings multiple times. However, each time you choose forgiveness, you reinforce your own emotional well-being.

4. **Engaging in Healing**: With forgiveness comes the opportunity to heal. Use this new emotional space to engage in activities that promote healing. Whether it's therapy, creative expression, or connecting with

nature, find what helps you heal and embrace it
fully.

While forgiveness can be liberally sprinkled with moments of profound relief and emotional liberation, it's also fraught with challenges. The process can stir up old emotions that you thought were resolved, leading to setbacks. You might find yourself revisiting feelings of anger or betrayal as you work through the layers of hurt. It's important to recognize that these setbacks are a normal part of your healing process. Patience with yourself and the situation is crucial.

Handling these challenges often requires additional strategies. For instance, practicing mindfulness can help you stay anchored in the present moment, reducing the power of past memories. Engaging in regular self-care activities can also provide emotional replenishment and resilience, supporting you through the lows of the forgiveness process. Additionally, seeking support from friends, family, or a therapist can provide you with a sounding board and emotional comfort when the process feels overwhelming.

Remember, forgiveness is a deeply personal and powerful tool for healing from trauma because it frees you from the chains of your past, allowing you to experience the present more fully and look towards the future with hope. By choosing forgiveness, you choose to honor your pain but not be defined by it, opening up a pathway to a renewed sense of peace and personal power. As you continue to explore and engage with this transformative process, remember that each step forward, no matter how small, is a step towards a more liberated and fulfilling life. We'll discuss forgiveness on a deeper level in Chapter 7.

THE ROLE OF PROFESSIONAL HELP IN EMOTIONAL HEALING

Getting through the aftermath of trauma can often feel like trying to find your way through a thick fog—directions are unclear, and the path forward is obscured. In such times, the guidance of a mental health professional is not just helpful but vital. These experts act as lighthouses, offering the light of their knowledge and experience to illuminate your journey through the healing process. They provide a safe space to explore your feelings, help you make sense of your experiences, and equip you with effective strategies to manage the emotional and psychological fallout of trauma.

Understanding the different roles of mental health professionals can help you determine who might be best suited to assist you based on your specific needs. Psychologists are trained to diagnose and treat a wide range of emotional and behavioral issues through counseling. They often specialize in certain areas such as clinical psychology, counseling, or child psychology, and are skilled in various forms of therapy including cognitive-behavioral therapy and psychoanalysis. Psychiatrists, on the other hand, are medical doctors who specialize in mental health and are qualified to prescribe medications. They can manage complex mental health conditions that might require pharmacological interventions alongside psychotherapy.

Counselors and social workers also play crucial roles in the mental health area. Counselors often focus on specific issues or demographic groups, such as marriage and family therapists who specialize in relationships, or addiction counselors who work with substance abuse issues. Social workers may provide more direct support, helping individuals to access resources and navigate systems that contribute to their well-being, in addition to offering therapeutic support. Each of these professionals brings a unique set of skills and perspectives to the table, making them valuable allies in your healing process.

Despite the clear benefits, many hesitate to seek professional help due to the stigma attached to mental health issues. Concerns about being perceived as weak or unstable, or fears about confidentiality, can prevent people from reaching out for the help they desperately need. It's important to recognize that seeking help is a sign of strength, not weakness. It shows a commitment to improving your well-being and a proactive approach to dealing with life's challenges. Mental health professionals are bound by strict confidentiality rules, meaning that the details of your situation are safe with them. They are there to support you, not to judge you.

If you're considering professional help, there are several resources to guide you in finding the right support. Start with a general visit to a primary care physician who can refer you to appropriate mental health professionals. Online directories and professional organizations related to mental health can also provide listings of qualified professionals in your area. Websites like Psychology Today allow you to search for therapists by location and specialty. Furthermore, support groups—

both in-person and online—can offer peer support and recommendations for therapists based on firsthand experiences.

Finding the right therapist or counselor requires knowing where you are, understanding where you want to go, and using the best resources to help you get there. Remember, the path to recovery from trauma is seldom straight; it involves making numerous adjustments and using various supports along the way. Professional guidance is an invaluable part of this process, providing you with the expertise and support needed to move forward towards healing.

In wrapping up this exploration of the role of professional help in emotional healing, remember that reaching out for help is a courageous step towards recovery. Mental health professionals not only offer critical guidance and support but also empower you with strategies and insights that facilitate a deeper understanding of your experiences and foster long-term healing. As we close this chapter, consider the strength that lies in seeking support and the profound impact it can have on your journey to recovery. Moving forward, the next chapter will discuss the transformative power of community support in healing, highlighting how connections with others can provide strength and foster resilience in the face of life's challenges.

FOSTERING SELF-COMPASSION AND FORGIVENESS

Our inner being consists of different facets. Some areas may look wild and shaded and others bright and vital, and other areas could benefit more from nurturing and kindness—particularly those neglected or overly criticized corners. In this chapter, we'll get into the practice of self-compassion, a crucial tool for nurturing the areas of ourselves that need the most care, enabling us to thrive emotionally and build healthier relationships with ourselves and others.

PRACTICING SELF-COMPANION: WHAT IT MEANS AND HOW TO START

Defining Self-Compassion

Self-compassion is an embracing approach where you offer yourself the same kindness, concern, and support you would offer a good friend. It arises from an understanding that everyone has moments of suffering, failure, and imperfection, which are inextricably part of the human experience. Kristin Neff, a leading researcher on self-compassion, suggests that treating ourselves compassionately can significantly alter the way we relate to ourselves and navigate challenges.

Explaining the Components of Self-Compassion

Self-compassion can be broken down into three main components: self-kindness, common humanity, and mindfulness.

- **Self-kindness** refers to the tendency to be caring and understanding with oneself rather than being harshly critical or judgmental. Instead of attacking yourself for personal failings, self-kindness allows you to be gentle and compassionate towards yourself. For instance, if you didn't perform as well as expected at work, instead of berating yourself with thoughts of "I'm not good enough," you might say, "I'm disappointed with how this went, but I'll learn from this experience."
- **Common humanity** involves recognizing that suffering and personal inadequacy are part of the shared human experience – something we all go through rather than being something that happens to "me" alone. This component helps you connect with others through your own experiences of struggle, fostering a sense of deep connection rather than isolation during difficult times.
- **Mindfulness** is the balanced approach we take to our negative emotions so that feelings are neither suppressed nor exaggerated. This balanced stance

stems from the process of relating personal experiences to those of others who are also suffering, thus putting our own situation into a larger perspective. It also stems from the willingness to observe our negative thoughts and emotions with openness and clarity, so that they are held in mindful awareness. Mindfulness allows you to notice your feelings without over-identifying with them or suppressing them, facilitating a perspective where you can approach your feelings with curiosity and compassion.

Introducing Beginner Exercises

To start practicing self-compassion, consider engaging in simple exercises such as writing a letter to yourself from the perspective of a compassionate friend or mentor. Address the challenges you're facing and respond with kindness, under-standing, and encouragement. Another exercise is to develop a set of compassionate phrases that you can say to yourself during difficult times, such as "May I give myself the compas-sion that I need," "May I learn to accept myself as I am," "May I forgive myself," and "May I be strong."

Discussing the Benefits of Self-Compassion

Engaging in self-compassion has profound benefits. It has been shown to increase overall emotional resilience, making you better equipped to handle stressful situations without falling into despair or overwhelming anxiety. People who practice self-compassion typically experience less anxiety and depression and report a higher quality of life. Moreover, by treating yourself with kindness and understanding, you're more likely to extend the same compassion towards others, enhancing your relationships and fostering a greater sense of connectedness.

By embracing self-compassion, you are taking a powerful step towards nurturing your emotional health and revitalizing your mind. As you practice self-kindness, recognize your common humanity, and maintain mindfulness of your experiences, you not only heal and strengthen yourself but also prepare the ground for deeper relationships and a fuller, more satisfying life.

THE HEALING POWER OF SELF-FORGIVENESS

In Chapter 6, we talked about the importance of forgiving others, but forgiving yourself is equally important. Self-forgiveness is an often misunderstood concept, tangled with notions of self-excusal and avoidance of responsibility. It's crucial to differentiate between forgiving oneself and excusing one's mistakes. Self-forgiveness is not about overlooking or justifying your errors but rather about releasing yourself from the paralyzing grip of self-blame. This distinction is vital because without self-forgiveness, you may remain trapped in a cycle of guilt and punishment that prevents healing and growth. When you forgive yourself, it doesn't mean you deny your mistakes or their impacts; instead, you acknowledge them and give yourself permission to move forward without the heavy burden of unresolved guilt. I personally believe, based on my personal experience, that this process will be less difficult when you develop a relationship with God, who loves us unconditionally.

Engaging in self-forgiveness is a step-by-step process that begins with the recognition and acknowledgment of your mistakes. This might be the hardest part, as it requires confronting aspects of yourself that you might not be proud of. However, this acknowledgment is essential for authentic growth. It involves a candid self-assessment where you admit to yourself where you went wrong and reflect on the reasons behind your actions. This process is not about inducing more guilt but about understanding and learning from your errors.

Once you have acknowledged your mistakes, the next step is to learn from them. This involves analyzing the situation and identifying what you could have done differently. The key here is to approach this phase with curiosity rather than judgment. By understanding the motivations behind your actions and the circumstances that influenced your decisions, you can gain insights that are crucial for your personal development. This learning phase transforms mistakes into valuable lessons that can inform your future choices and interactions, reducing the likelihood of repeating the same errors.

Making amends where possible is also an integral part of self-forgiveness. If your actions have hurt others, seeking to rectify those wrongs can be a powerful step towards healing. This might involve apologizing to someone you've wronged or making efforts to compensate for the damage caused. However, it's important to recognize that making amends is not always about seeking forgiveness from others but about doing what you believe is right and responsible. This action reaffirms your commitment to living according to your values and helps restore your sense of integrity.

The role of self-forgiveness in personal growth is profound as it liberates you from the shackles of past mistakes, allowing you to embrace a future where you are not defined by your errors. By forgiving yourself, you foster a mindset of learning and growth rather than one of punishment and regret. This shift is crucial for developing resilience and a more compassionate self-view. It encourages you to view challenges and setbacks as opportunities for growth and self-discovery, rather than as insurmountable obstacles.

Reflective Questions for Personal Growth

To further facilitate your process of self-forgiveness, consider engaging with the following reflective questions. These are designed to help you delve deeper into understanding your actions and their impacts, and to foster a forgiving attitude towards yourself:

1. **What are the mistakes for which I still blame myself?**
2. Identify specific instances where you have not yet forgiven yourself. Articulate what happened and why you feel responsible.
3. **What were the circumstances and factors that led to these mistakes?**
4. Reflect on the context in which these mistakes were made. Consider external pressures, emotional states,

or knowledge gaps that may have influenced your decisions.

5. **How have these mistakes affected my view of myself?**

6. Consider how these errors have shaped your self-perception. Are you holding on to labels like "failure" or "incompetent"?

7. **What have I learned from these experiences, and how can I apply these lessons moving forward?**

8. Extract key lessons from each mistake and think about how these insights can guide your future actions and decisions.

9. **What steps can I take to make amends for my actions?**

10. List concrete actions you can take to address the consequences of your mistakes, whether through apologies, reparations, or changed behavior.

Engaging deeply with these questions can be a transformative experience, providing you with the insights needed to move forward with a lighter heart and a clearer conscience. As you go through the process of self-forgiveness, remember that it's not about erasing the past but about learning from it and making peace with it. This approach not only enhances your relationship with yourself but also equips you to handle future challenges with greater wisdom and compassion.

EXTENDING FORGIVENESS TO OTHERS TO RELEASE EMOTIONAL BONDS

As we mentioned before, forgiving others is often miscon-strued as a sign of weakness or as an absolution of someone's wrongdoing. But, in reality, forgiveness is a powerful act of self-liberation from the grip of past grievances that can skew your present emotional health. It isn't about validating the wrongs done to you but rather about choosing to release the heavy burden of resentment. This act of letting go is crucial, not for the benefit of the person who wronged you, but for your peace of mind and emotional freedom. Resentment can be likened to drinking poison and expecting the other person to suffer; it only harms the bearer, tying them to negative emotions and memories that impede happiness and emotional wellbeing.

However, the path to forgiveness is often blocked by substan-tial barriers. Feelings of injustice or betrayal can anchor the heart in anger and prevent it from moving forward. The pain of being wronged, especially by someone you trusted, can leave deep emotional scars, making the idea of forgiveness seem impossible or even undeserved. Overcoming these barriers requires a shift in perspective and a commitment to personal peace. One effective strategy is reframing the situation to understand the broader context of the person's actions. It's helpful to consider questions like: What struggles might they have been facing? Could their actions have been a misguided attempt to deal with their pain? This isn't about excusing their behavior but about understanding it from a broader perspective, which can sometimes soften the harsh edges of resentment.

Building empathy is a critical step in this process. It involves seeing beyond your emotional response and stepping into the shoes of the other person. Techniques to cultivate empathy include reflecting on times when you might have wronged someone out of ignorance or pain and considering how you wished to be forgiven. Understanding that everyone is capable of making mistakes, often driven by their unresolved issues or pressures, can open a pathway to empathy. Another method is the 'perspective-taking' exercise where you actively attempt to view the situation from the other person's angle, considering their emotions, background, and pressures that might have influenced their actions.

To facilitate the process of forgiveness, practical exercises can be very effective. Writing a forgiveness letter is a powerful tool, even if you choose not to send it. In this letter, express all your feelings about the situation and how it impacted you. Articulate your understanding of the other person's perspective, and then explicitly state your intention to forgive them. This exercise can be profoundly cathartic, allowing you to express your emotions fully and to symbolically let go of them. Another helpful exercise is the visualization of releasing emotional baggage. Close your eyes and imagine packing all your feelings of hurt, betrayal, and anger into a suitcase. Visualize yourself walking to a place of peace, and with each step, feel the weight of the suitcase getting lighter until you arrive and can leave the suitcase behind, walking away unburdened. Another method that is very effective includes writing your negative feelings of unforgiveness on a piece of paper and burning it (do this outside in a safe, controlled environment). This act of *detaching* yourself from the negative feelings and sense of guilt is very effective. I had practiced this in workshops and everyone felt the difference between how they were feeling before the exercise and after the exercise.

Through these methods, forgiveness becomes a feasible and enriching path. It allows you to reclaim your emotional space and energy, redirecting them from past hurts to present healing and future joys. As you practice forgiveness, whether through empathy exercises, writing, or visualization, you'll likely discover a growing sense of peace and *emotional liberation*. This newfound freedom not only enhances your wellbeing but also enriches your interactions with others, opening up a space for healthier and more fulfilling relationships. By choosing forgiveness, you choose to prioritize your emotional health and peace, setting a foundation for a more compassionate and resilient emotional life.

OVERCOMING SELF-CRITICISM THROUGH AFFIRMATIVE PRACTICES

At the heart of personal development lies the often-overlooked issue of self-criticism. While it's natural to evaluate one's actions, excessive self-criticism can spiral into a destructive cycle, severely affecting emotional health and stifling personal growth. This self-inflicted scrutiny can manifest in persistent doubts and negative self-talk, which not only dampens self-esteem but can also lead to significant mental health issues like anxiety and depression. Moreover, it can cripple your ability to pursue and achieve personal and professional goals, as you become entangled in a web of paralyzing fear of failure and rejection.

To combat the harmful effects of self-criticism, it's essential to adopt affirmative practices. These practices are designed to nurture a more positive and forgiving dialogue with oneself. *Positive affirmations*, as mentioned before, are powerful tools in this endeavor. These are constructive, first-person statements that are repeated to oneself, designed to foster self-acceptance and counter negative thoughts. For example, instead of succumbing to the critic within that insists "I'm not good enough," affirmations encourage a supportive narrative such as "I am capable and resilient." By regularly affirming your worth and abilities, you gradually reshape the mental pathways associated with self-perception.

Another effective practice is *gratitude journaling*. This involves regularly writing down things for which you are thankful for, ranging from simple joys like a sunny day to significant achievements such as completing a project. This practice helps shift focus from what's lacking or has gone wrong to what's abundant and right in your life, fostering a sense of contentment and reducing the urge to criticize oneself harshly.

Another transformative practice is *strength-spotting* where you actively identify and celebrate your personal strengths. It involves recognizing your abilities, not just in terms of what you achieve but also how you navigate challenges and setbacks. Acknowledging your resilience in facing past difficulties, your creativity in problem-solving, or your empathy in dealing with others helps build a self-image that's rooted in competence and kindness rather than in perceived failings.

Developing a *positive self-dialogue* is crucial in mitigating self-criticism. This process begins with becoming aware of the critical inner voice and consciously choosing to engage with it differently. When you catch yourself spiraling into self-criticism, pause and challenge these thoughts. Ask yourself, "Is this really true?" or "Would I talk to someone I care about this way?" Often, you'll find that your criticisms are harsher than what you would ever express to others. By reframing these thoughts into more compassionate and constructive feedback, you gradually learn to be kinder to yourself.

Moreover, *regular reflection on your thoughts and feelings* plays a vital role in this transformation. Set aside time each day or week to reflect on situations where you noticed your critical inner voice was most active. Consider what triggered these thoughts, how they made you feel, and how you responded. Reflect on what these patterns might be telling you about your needs and expectations. This ongoing reflection enhances your self-awareness and helps you develop healthier ways to relate to yourself.

Embracing these affirmative practices does not mean ignoring areas where you need to improve. Instead, it's about shifting from a critical to a supportive approach in personal growth. Instead of letting self-criticism hold you back, use positive affirmations, gratitude journaling, and strength-spotting to foster resilience and a more compassionate self-view. Through these practices, you not only enhance your well-being but also set a solid foundation for achieving your personal and professional goals.

As we wrap up this exploration of strategies to counter self-criticism, it's clear that fostering a supportive and forgiving internal dialogue is crucial for both personal well-being and effective engagement with the world. The practices discussed not only help mitigate the harshness of self-criticism but also enhance your capacity to appreciate and leverage your innate strengths. Moving forward, the next chapter will focus on building and maintaining healthy relationships, a natural extension of the work done here. By understanding and improving how we relate to ourselves, we lay the groundwork for more fulfilling and supportive interactions with others.

ESTABLISHING AND MAINTAINING HEALTHY RELATIONSHIPS

A sense of harmony and connection isn't just vital for a music concert but is the essence of what builds and sustains healthy relationships. Whether it's with a friend, family member, or partner, the quality of your relationships profoundly influences your emotional health and overall well-being. In this chapter, we'll explore the core qualities that constitute healthy relationships, the importance of emotional availability, and how shared values and interests can strengthen bonds, providing real-life examples to illustrate these concepts.

QUALITIES OF HEALTHY RELATIONSHIPS: WHAT TO LOOK FOR

Identifying Core Qualities

The foundation of any healthy relationship is built on several core qualities: *trust, honesty, support, and affection*. Each of these qualities plays a crucial role in fostering a secure and positive relationship environment. Trust, the cornerstone of all relationships, involves believing that the other person will act with respect and integrity towards you. It's the security that allows you to feel safe and open in sharing your thoughts and feelings. Honesty, closely tied to trust, is about being truthful and transparent. It fosters a genuine understanding and helps avoid misunderstandings that could lead to conflict.

Support in relationships manifests through emotional encouragement, understanding, and practical help. It's knowing that someone has your back, whether you're facing a stressful day or celebrating a personal achievement. Affection, expressed through words, gestures, or actions, reinforces a sense of love and care between individuals, nurturing the emotional connection that bonds people together.

Highlighting the Value of Emotional Availability

Emotional availability in both partners is essential for a deep and meaningful connection. It involves being present and responsive to each other's emotional needs. When both individuals in a relationship can share their feelings openly and receive empathetic responses, it strengthens the bond and provides a solid foundation for dealing with challenges together. Emotional availability also allows for vulnerability, where both partners feel safe to express their fears, disappointments, and hopes, fostering a deeper level of intimacy and understanding.

The Role of Shared Values and Interests

Having aligned values and interests can significantly enhance the strength and enjoyment of a relationship. Shared values, such as beliefs about family, work ethic, or personal growth, provide a common framework that guides decisions and behaviors within the relationship. Interests, whether in hobbies, sports, or arts, offer opportunities for bonding, creating shared experiences, and making memories. When partners participate in activities they both enjoy, it not only brings fun and relaxation into the relationship but also builds a layer of companionship and friendship that is vital for long-term satisfaction.

Real-Life Examples and Case Studies

Consider the story of Maya and Alex, a couple who credit their strong relationship to their shared value of adventure and their mutual interest in travel. Their journeys together have not only enriched their lives with unforgettable experiences but have also allowed them to go through challenges and support each other in times of need, reinforcing their bond. Another example is that of Raj and Sam, who, despite their different backgrounds, found common ground in their values of family and loyalty. Their commitment to these shared values has helped them foster a relationship that is supportive and enduring, even when faced with external pressures.

These examples illustrate how the core qualities of trust, honesty, support, and affection, combined with emotional availability and shared values, are instrumental in building and maintaining healthy relationships. They highlight the profound impact these factors have on the individuals involved, enhancing their emotional well-being and enriching their lives. As we continue to explore the dynamics of effective communication and mutual respect in the following sections, keep in mind the foundational qualities discussed here, as they are integral to the art of building relationships that are not only healthy but also joyous and fulfilling.

COMMUNICATING EFFECTIVELY WITH EMPATHY

Empathetic communication is akin to tuning into a radio frequency where both parties are fully engaged in truly understanding each other's broadcasts, clear and free from interference. This form of communication is foundational in strengthening connections by fostering a deep sense of understanding and support between each other. When you communicate empathetically, you're not just exchanging information; you're actively participating in the emotional landscape of the conversation, which enhances the bond and trust in any relationship. Empathy involves putting yourself in someone else's shoes, understanding their feelings and perspectives without judgment, and responding with compassion and sincerity.

One of the most effective ways to develop empathetic communication is through honing your active listening skills. Active listening is about fully concentrating on what is being said rather than just passively hearing the message of the speaker. Techniques such as maintaining eye contact signal to the speaker that you are fully focused and engaged, creating a sense of respect and value for what they are sharing. Paraphrasing, or repeating back what the speaker has said in your own words, is another crucial technique. It shows that you are not only listening but also processing the information, which can help clarify any misunderstandings in real-time. Additionally, asking open-ended questions that encourage elaboration rather than simple yes or no answers can deepen the conversation, providing greater insight into the emotions and thoughts behind the words shared.

Encouraging emotional expression is another key aspect of empathetic communication. In any relationship, the ability to express emotions openly and safely is vital for the health and longevity of the connection. It is important to create an environment where all parties feel secure in sharing their true feelings without fear of dismissal or ridicule. This can be established through verbal affirmations that acknowledge and validate the emotions being expressed, such as saying, "I really appreciate you sharing this with me," or "It sounds like that was really difficult for you." These affirmations help to reinforce a supportive environment and demonstrate genuine care and interest in the emotional well-being of those involved.

To further enhance empathetic communication, consider engaging in practical exercises designed to strengthen these skills. Role-reversal scenarios, for example, are a dynamic way to practice empathy. By stepping into someone else's role and perspective, you gain firsthand insight into their emotional experience, which can illuminate misunderstandings and deepen empathy. Another effective exercise is engaging in empathy-building activities that focus on shared experiences. These activities could involve discussing a movie or book in which characters undergo emotional challenges and reflecting together on how you each related to the characters' experiences. Through shared dialogue, you can explore different emotional reactions and perspectives, which enhances mutual understanding and empathy.

Incorporating these techniques and exercises into your daily interactions can transform the way you communicate and connect with others. By practicing active listening, encouraging emotional expression, and engaging in empathy-building activities, you foster an environment where meaningful and supportive relationships can thrive. These methods not only enhance personal relationships but also improve interactions in professional settings, contributing to a more compassionate and understanding community. As we continue to explore the nuances of effective communication, remember that the core of all strong relationships is the genuine effort to understand and connect with one another at a deep emotional level.

If you would like to learn more about *effective communication skills*, check out the author's book: *"The Power of Communication Skills and Effective Listening: Say What You Mean and Mean What You Say"* available on Amazon.

THE IMPORTANCE OF MUTUAL RESPECT AND HOW TO CULTIVATE IT

Respect is often likened to the cement that holds the bricks of a relationship together; without it, the structure is weak and liable to crumble under pressure. In the context of any healthy relationship, mutual respect is fundamental. It acts as a powerful force that enhances communication, deepens trust, and promotes a sense of safety and belonging. When respect is present, each person in the relationship feels valued and understood, which naturally enhances the relationship's dynamics. However, maintaining this respect is not always automatic; it requires conscious effort and understanding.

One of the most common pitfalls that can erode respect is dismissiveness. When one person constantly minimizes or disregards the other person's feelings, opinions, or needs, it sends a message that these aspects are unimportant. This behavior can deeply hurt the dismissed person, leading to resentment and a breakdown in communication. Contempt, another respect-destroying behavior, involves treating the other with disdain or scorn, often manifested through sarcasm, cynicism, name-calling, or eye-rolling. Such actions are not only disrespectful but deeply damaging, as they attack the individual's sense of self-worth. Over-criticism, where one partner persistently criticizes the other, often focusing on their flaws instead of their strengths, can also diminish respect, leading to a defensive environment rather than one of mutual support.

To avoid these pitfalls, it is important to foster habits that build and maintain respect. One such habit is *the consistent expression of appreciation*. This involves regularly acknowledging and expressing gratitude for the other person's actions, qualities, or presence in your life. It's about noticing the small things they do and letting them know how much these actions are valued. Recognition of each other's contributions to the relationship or household can also play a significant role in fostering respect. Whether it's acknowledging a partner's effort in managing the household, recognizing their success at work, or appreciating their support during a tough time, these recognitions reinforce the value each person brings to the relationship.

Handling disagreements constructively is another critical area in building respect. Disagreements are natural in any relationship, but the way they are managed can either strengthen or weaken respect. It's important to approach conflicts with a mindset of finding a solution rather than winning an argument. This involves listening actively, acknowledging the other person's perspective, and working together to find a compromise that respects both parties' needs. Avoiding blame and instead focusing on how to resolve the issue not only preserves respect but also builds a stronger partnership.

Self-respect is the bedrock upon which mutual respect is built. When you hold yourself in high regard, it sets the standard for how others should treat you. Enhancing your self-respect can be achieved through several practices. First, engage in activities that foster a sense of accomplishment and pride. Whether it's pursuing a hobby, advancing your career, or volunteering, these activities build self-esteem, which is essential for self-respect. Additionally, setting personal boundaries and sticking to them can significantly enhance self-respect. This might mean saying 'no' to additional responsibilities when you're already stretched thin or choosing to spend time alone to recharge. When you respect your own limits and needs, you're better able to interact in ways that promote respect within your relationships.

In cultivating these habits, remember that respect is not just about grand gestures; it's built in the small, everyday interactions. Each respectful exchange, no matter how minor it may seem, contributes to a stronger, more resilient relationship foundation. By consistently practicing appreciation, recognizing each other's contributions, handling disagreements constructively, and fostering self-respect, you create an environment where mutual respect thrives. These practices not only enhance personal relationships but also model respectful behavior that can influence others, contributing to a more respectful and understanding society. Through conscious effort and dedication, respect can become the default mode of operation, transforming not only personal relationships but also the broader interactions we encounter daily.

NURTURING CONNECTIONS: KEEPING RELATIONSHIPS HEALTHY

Maintaining a healthy relationship involves regular, proactive efforts to nurture the bond between individuals, ensuring the relationship remains vibrant and fulfilling over time. *Scheduled check-ins*, for instance, can be an invaluable strategy. These are designated times—perhaps over a weekly dinner or a monthly walk in the park—where you and your partner, or you and a close friend, can discuss what's going well in your relationship and what might need more attention. This open line of communication helps prevent small issues from growing into larger conflicts and reinforces the importance of the relationship in each person's life.

Moreover, engaging in shared activities can significantly enhance relationship health. Whether it's a hobby that both parties enjoy, a class you take together, or a project you collaborate on, shared activities create opportunities for fun, teamwork, and creating new memories together. These experiences not only bring joy and closeness but also reinforce the partnership by working towards common goals and enjoying each other's company in diverse settings. This aspect of relationship maintenance is crucial because it injects fresh energy into the relationship, keeping the dynamic lively and engaging.

Continual growth, both individually and as a couple, is another pillar of keeping relationships healthy. Encouraging each other's personal development and pursuing growth together can greatly enhance the quality of the relationship. For individuals, personal growth might involve pursuing a new educational goal, developing a new skill, or focusing on personal health. Supporting each other in these individual pursuits not only shows care and respect for each other's personal goals but also brings new energy and insights into the relationship. On a collective level, growth might look like setting relationship goals, such as improving communication, planning for future financial stability, or cultivating a shared hobby. These shared endeavors not only bring you closer but also ensure that the relationship evolves in a way that meets the needs and aspirations of both parties.

Handling changes is an inevitable part of any long-term relationship. As individuals grow, relationships must adapt to new circumstances, perspectives, and challenges. This might include changes like moving to a new city, changing career paths, or adjusting to a new family dynamic. Navigating these changes together requires flexibility, open communication, and a willingness to renegotiate terms that may no longer serve the relationship well. It's about finding ways to adapt together, ensuring that the relationship remains a source of support and happiness amidst life's inevitable transitions. For instance, if one partner needs to relocate for a job, discussing ways to maintain connection and intimacy can help manage the change more effectively, such as setting regular communication schedules or planning frequent visits.

Sometimes, even the strongest relationships can hit a plateau, where things might start to feel routine or stagnant. When this happens, rekindling the connection is crucial. This can be achieved by rediscovering each other's evolving interests and goals. Perhaps your partner has developed a new interest in photography or you've found a renewed passion for hiking. Engaging with each other's new hobbies or interests can revitalize the relationship by adding new layers of understanding and appreciation. Planning surprises, revisiting places that hold special memories, or creating new traditions can also inject new vitality into the relationship. These efforts show your commitment to keeping the relationship dynamic and responsive to the ever-changing nature of each person's passions and dreams.

In essence, nurturing connections in relationships is about commitment to growth, adaptability, and the joyful pursuit of shared experiences. It's about ensuring that the relationship's soil remains fertile, allowing the bond to deepen and flourish over time. By regularly investing time and energy into maintaining and enriching these connections, you ensure that your relationships not only survive but thrive, adapting gracefully to whatever life brings your way.

SETTING AND RESPECTING BOUNDARIES IN RELATIONSHIPS

Boundaries in relationships function much like lines on a map delineating one state from another; they help define where one person's territory ends and another's begins. In regards to relationships, boundaries are the explicit or implied limits that individuals set to protect their emotional, physical, and mental well-being. These boundaries can vary significantly depending on the nature of the relationship. For instance, the boundaries you set with a partner are likely to be different from those you set with colleagues or friends, reflecting the different levels of intimacy and interaction.

Establishing boundaries is not about building walls but about bridging understanding. To effectively set boundaries, start by identifying your limits. What makes you feel comfortable and safe? Reflecting on your values and experiences can help clarify these limits. Once you know what boundaries you need, communicate them clearly and respectfully. For example, if you decide you need more time alone to recharge, you might say to your partner, "I value our time together, but I also need some time to myself to stay balanced. Can we plan some quiet time for me in our weekly schedule?" This approach is direct yet considerate, emphasizing the importance of your needs while respecting the relationship's dynamics.

When communicating your boundaries, use "I" statements to express your feelings and needs without blaming or criticizing the other person. This method fosters a more receptive environment for understanding and lessens the likelihood of defensive reactions. Be as specific as possible about what is okay and what isn't, and explain why the boundary is important to you. This clarity reduces misunderstandings and provides a strong foundation for mutual respect.

Respecting others' boundaries is just as crucial as establishing your own. It involves recognizing and honoring the other person's limits, just as you expect yours to be respected. This practice is fundamental to sustaining trust and safety within relationships. It shows a commitment to the health of the relationship and demonstrates empathy and consideration for the other person's feelings and needs.

However, boundary violations can and do occur, sometimes unintentionally. This is very common within family dynamics. Common violations include overstepping emotional boundaries, such as prying into personal matters without consent, or physical boundaries, like unsolicited physical contact. When these breaches happen, addressing them promptly and effectively is key to maintaining healthy interactions. Start by clearly identifying the violation and expressing how it affected you, using "I" statements to communicate your feelings. For instance, if a friend shares private information about you without permission, you might say, "*I felt* hurt when you discussed my health issues without asking me first. *I value* our friendship and trust, and it's important to me that my privacy is respected."

If boundary violations persist despite clear communication, it may be necessary to enforce consequences, such as taking a step back from the relationship or seeking external support from a counselor or mediator. This isn't about punishment but about protecting your well-being and reinforcing the seriousness of your boundaries.

In navigating these interactions, remember that setting and respecting boundaries is a dynamic process that requires ongoing attention and adjustment. As relationships grow and change, so too might the necessary boundaries. Regular check-ins can help ensure that everyone's needs are being met and that the boundaries are still serving their intended purpose.

In this chapter, we discussed the critical role that setting and respecting boundaries plays in maintaining healthy relationships. By understanding the importance of boundaries, learning how to establish and communicate them effectively, and addressing violations constructively, you equip yourself with the tools necessary to foster respectful and fulfilling connections. As we move forward, these principles will not only enhance your personal relationships but also empower you to navigate the broader spectrum of interactions in your life with confidence and clarity.

PREVENTING RELAPSE INTO TOXIC PATTERNS

*a*s weeds can quickly take over your lawn if not addressed, so can toxic emotional patterns re-emerge in your life, even after you've done significant work to eradicate them. This chapter is dedicated to helping you recognize the early signs of such emotional relapse and providing you with the strategies to maintain the health of your emotional state of mind.

RECOGNIZING EARLY WARNING SIGNS OF TOXICITY

The first step in maintaining your emotional health is recognizing the subtle signs that toxic patterns may be resurfacing. These signs can often be as subtle as a feeling of unease, a return to old, unhealthy coping mechanisms, or an increase in negativity. You might find yourself reverting to short-tempered responses in stress, withdrawing from loved ones, or feeling a persistent sense of powerlessness or sadness. These emotions and behaviors can serve as early warning signals, indicating that your emotional well-being is under threat.

Vigilance is your greatest ally in recognizing these signs. It requires a continuous, conscious awareness of your emotional state. This might sound demanding, but it becomes more manageable when you make it a part of your routine. During periods of major life transitions or stress—times when you are most vulnerable to relapse—it's particularly crucial to monitor your emotional health closely. For example, if you're starting a new job, moving to a new city, or going through a breakup, these are prime times to be on high alert for signs of toxic patterns creeping back into your life.

One effective tool to aid in this vigilance is *maintaining a daily mood log*. This can be as simple as jotting down a few notes on your phone or keeping a more detailed journal. Each day, record your emotional state along with any thoughts or events that might be influencing your mood. Tracking these patterns over time can help you connect the dots between certain triggers and your emotional responses to them. This log will not only help you recognize toxic patterns but also empower you to understand what precipitates these states, which is crucial for addressing them effectively.

Moreover, the role of a trusted confidant cannot be overstated. Sometimes, having an external observer can provide a perspective that is difficult to see from within. This could be a friend, family member, or a therapist—someone you trust who can help you notice patterns you might miss and provide an outside perspective on changes in your behavior. They can act as a mirror, reflecting back to you what they see, which can sometimes be the key to recognizing your own toxic patterns before they take root again.

STRATEGIES FOR SUSTAINING CHANGE: KEEPING TOXIC EMOTIONS AT BAY

As you continue to deal with your emotions, remember to apply the coping strategies you've learned to your daily routine to ensure they hold strong against the pull of old habits and toxic patterns.

Mindfulness, for example, is not just a practice but a way of living that requires consistent engagement. It involves being present in the moment and accepting your thoughts and feelings without judgment.

Similarly, *assertive communication* must be practiced regularly to become a natural part of how you interact with others. It involves expressing your thoughts and feelings openly and respectfully, regardless of the situation. To embed this into your daily interactions, start by identifying scenarios where you typically struggle to communicate assertively. Set small, achievable goals for each situation. For instance, if you tend to be passive during meetings, you might aim to express at least one of your ideas or opinions in the next meeting. Gradually, as you become more comfortable, increase your contributions. This gradual escalation allows you to build confidence in your ability to communicate effectively, reinforcing the practice of assertive communication.

Setting boundaries is another crucial strategy for maintaining emotional health. Boundaries help define what is acceptable and what is not, protecting your emotional space from being compromised. To reinforce this practice, regularly assess and adjust your boundaries based on your current emotional needs, which can change over time. For example, if you find that spending too much time on social media is impacting your mood negatively, you might decide to set stricter boundaries around your usage. Communicate these boundaries clearly to those around you and stick to them, adjusting as necessary to ensure they continue to serve your best interests.

The *development of healthy habits* plays a pivotal role in sustaining the changes you've made in managing toxic emotions. Regular physical activity, adequate sleep, and balanced nutrition are foundational habits that support overall emotional health. Physical activity, in particular, is not only beneficial for your physical health but also for your mental well-being. It releases endorphins, which have mood-boosting properties. Aim to integrate some form of physical activity into your daily routine, whether it's a morning jog, a yoga session, or a brisk walk during your lunch break. Similarly, ensuring you get enough sleep and eat a balanced diet are crucial for maintaining your energy levels and mood stability.

Positive reinforcement is a powerful tool in sustaining behavioral changes. It involves rewarding yourself for successfully managing potentially toxic situations using the strategies you've learned. These rewards can be anything that feels like a treat to you, such as a small purchase, an extra episode of your favorite show, or a special meal. The act of rewarding yourself helps to cement the positive behaviors you're developing, making it more likely that you'll continue to use them in the future as these rewards not only serve as motivation to maintain your efforts but also provide a tangible acknowledgment of your hard work and progress.

Adapting these strategies over time is essential to their effectiveness. As your life circumstances change, so too will your emotional needs and challenges. Regularly review the strategies you are using to ensure they remain relevant and effective. This might involve tweaking your mindfulness practice, finding new ways to apply assertive communication, or setting new boundaries. The key is to remain flexible and responsive to your changing needs, ensuring that your strategies for managing toxic emotions evolve along with you.

By consistently applying these strategies, promoting healthy habits, and using positive reinforcement, you can effectively sustain the changes you've made in your journey to overcoming toxic emotions. This ongoing commitment to your emotional well-being is not just about preventing relapse but about fostering a life that is vibrant, fulfilling, and resilient.

ROLE OF LIFESTYLE IN PREVENTING EMOTIONAL TOXICITY

Your daily lifestyle choices play an instrumental role in shaping your emotional well-being. Every action, from what you eat and how often you move, to the ways you choose to spend your free time, plays an important role in your mental health. Let's take a look at how these elements not only contribute to your overall health but specifically act as pivotal factors in maintaining your emotional stability and guarding against the resurgence of toxic emotions.

Diet, often overlooked in discussions about emotional health, is foundational. What you consume can affect your brain chemistry and, consequently, your moods and emotions. For instance, foods high in omega-3 fatty acids, like salmon and flaxseeds, are known to enhance brain function and could potentially lower the symptoms of depression. On the other hand, excessive intake of sugar and processed foods can lead to fluctuations in blood sugar levels, which may trigger mood swings and irritability. Therefore, integrating a balanced diet rich in fruits, vegetables, lean proteins, and whole grains can help stabilize your mood and fortify your emotional resilience. Think of your diet as fuel for both your body and mind, where nutritious foods act like high-quality gasoline that keeps everything running smoothly and efficiently.

Exercise is another pillar of a lifestyle that supports emotional health. Engaging in regular physical activity is not just about maintaining physical fitness; it's about keeping your mental state in check. Exercise releases endorphins, often referred to as feel-good hormones, which can create feelings of happiness and euphoria. Even beyond endorphins, regular physical activity can help regulate your body's stress hormones, such as adrenaline and cortisol, keeping them from overwhelming you. But the benefits don't stop at biochemical processes. Exercise also provides a constructive outlet for frustration and anxiety. Whether it's a brisk walk, a run, a dance class, or even gardening, these activities can serve as a physical dialogue with your body, telling it to maintain calm and resilience in the face of life's challenges.

Balancing your lifestyle is about more than just what you eat and how you move. It involves creating a rhythm to your day that allows for work, relaxation, social interaction, and solitude. Each of these elements plays a critical role in emotional health. Work provides a sense of purpose and accomplishment, relaxation allows for mental and physical recovery, social interactions offer emotional support and connection, and solitude gives space for self-reflection and growth. Striking a balance among these can prevent feelings of burnout and isolation, which often accompany or trigger toxic emotional states. It's about creating a daily routine where these elements harmonize rather than compete, ensuring that no single aspect overwhelms the others. For instance, you might structure your day to include dedicated work hours, set times for breaks and relaxation, regular slots for socializing, and quiet time for yourself. This not only helps in managing stress but also in fostering a sense of control and predictability, which can be incredibly reassuring in a chaotic world.

Lastly, *engaging regularly in activities* that bring joy is crucial. Joy is a powerful antidote to emotional toxicity. It's essential to identify what activities make you feel alive, content, or excited, and to incorporate them into your life regularly. These could be hobbies like painting, writing, or playing a musical instrument, or simple pleasures like watching a favorite show, reading a book, or spending time with loved ones. The key is consistency and intentionality—making sure that these activities are not random afterthoughts but integral parts of your weekly or even daily schedule. By regularly engaging in these joy-inducing activities, you build a buffer against the negative emotions and stress that life inevitably brings. They keep the darkness at bay, fill your emotional reserves, and remind you of the beauty and positivity that life has to offer, even when times are tough.

Incorporating these lifestyle elements effectively requires mindfulness and commitment. It's about making conscious choices every day that align with emotional well-being. Just like a garden, your emotional state of mind needs regular tending—active living, balanced routines, nutritious foods, and joyful engagements are the water and sunlight it needs to thrive. By cultivating these habits, you not only prevent the weeds of toxicity from taking root but also ensure that your mental health remains a place of beauty and peace.

MAINTAINING EMOTIONAL CLARITY: REGULAR SELF-ASSESSMENT TOOLS

In regards to your emotional health, self-awareness is akin to guide you through the ups and down states of your mind. Without regular checkpoints and moments of reflection, it's easy to veer off course, losing sight of your progress and potentially falling back into old, destructive patterns. Self-assessment tools are your markers along this path, offering you the opportunity to pause, evaluate, and recalibrate your emotional state and strategies. These tools—ranging from emotional check-ins and reflection journals to structured mindfulness practices—are not just methods for assessment but are also practices in mindfulness and personal accountability.

Incorporating tools such as *emotional check-ins* into your daily routine can serve as both a preventive measure against emotional overwhelm and a barometer for your emotional well-being. An emotional check-in involves taking a few moments each day to pause and reflect on your feelings *and the reasons behind them*. This practice can be as simple as setting a daily alarm as a reminder to pause, breathe, and mentally review the emotions you've experienced throughout the day. Over time, this habit fosters a heightened awareness of your emotional triggers and responses, allowing you to recognize patterns or shifts in your emotional state before they escalate into larger issues.

Reflection journals offer a more detailed exploration of your thoughts and emotions. By regularly writing down your feelings, reactions to daily events, and personal reflections, you create a historical record of your emotional evolution. This process not only aids in catharsis but also serves as a tool for deeper analysis of your emotional triggers and patterns over time. As you review your entries, you can identify recurring themes or issues, providing insights into areas that may require more focused attention or adjustment in your coping strategies.

Integrating mindfulness practices into your daily routine enhances both emotional clarity and resilience. Mindfulness involves maintaining a moment-by-moment awareness of our thoughts, feelings, bodily sensations, and surrounding environment through a gentle, nurturing lens. Practices such as guided meditations, mindful breathing exercises, or even mindful walking are accessible ways to cultivate a state of mindfulness. These practices help center your thoughts, calm your mind, and ground you in the present moment, reducing feelings of stress and anxiety while increasing your overall sense of well-being. The key is consistency. Over time, this practice helps in recognizing the onset of toxic emotions and provides you with the space to choose how you respond, rather than reacting impulsively.

Reflective questions are another powerful tool in your self-assessment arsenal. These questions should be designed to provoke thought and self-exploration, allowing you to evaluate your emotional health and alignment with your personal goals. Questions might include: How do I feel about my personal growth over the past month? What emotions have I found challenging recently, and why? How effectively am I using my coping strategies, and in what situations do I find them most helpful? By regularly contemplating these questions, you engage in an ongoing dialogue with yourself about your emotional needs and achievements, fostering a deeper under-standing of your mental health landscape.

Setting regular intervals for formal reviews of your emotional goals and achievements is crucial for sustained emotional management. This practice involves scheduling monthly or quarterly sessions to sit down and systematically review your emotional journal entries, responses to reflective questions, and overall progress toward your emotional goals. These reviews allow you to celebrate successes, identify areas for improvement, and adjust your strategies to better meet your needs. They also provide a structured opportunity to reflect on your emotional journey and the growth you've achieved, reinforcing your commitment to maintaining your emotional health.

Emotional Awareness Exercise

To enhance your ability to recognize early signs of toxicity, engage in this simple yet effective exercise:

- **Daily Emotional Check-In**: Set a daily reminder to assess your emotional state. Rate your overall mood on a scale from 1 to 10, and note any predominant emotions you feel. Reflect on what might be influencing your mood that day.
- **Journaling Prompt**: Once a week, spend some time writing about any patterns you've noticed in your mood log. Are there specific days, situations, or interactions that consistently impact your mood? How do these align with the toxic patterns you've previously encountered?
- **Confidant Feedback**: Monthly, have a check-in with your trusted confidant. Discuss your observations and get their perspective on your emotional state and behaviors.

Engaging regularly in these practices can sharpen your awareness and help you catch toxic patterns early, making it easier to address them before they escalate. This proactive approach to emotional health keeps your mind flourishing, free from the weeds of toxicity and empower yourself with the knowledge and skills necessary to maintain clarity about your emotional state. They enable you to remain aligned with your path toward emotional well-being and resilience and integral parts of your daily routine, contributing significantly to your overall mental health and stability.

CREATING A PERSONALIZED EMOTIONAL SAFETY PLAN

An emotional safety plan is a carefully crafted tool that acts as your personal guide to managing emotional health, especially in times of stress or crisis. Think of it as a blueprint that outlines the specific steps you can take to protect your emotional well-being during challenging times. This proactive approach is not merely about coping but thriving, ensuring you have a clear strategy to maintain emotional stability, even when the waters get rough.

The creation of your personalized emotional safety plan begins with the identification of triggers—those situations, people, or emotions that can potentially destabilize your mental state. Start by reflecting on past experiences where you felt overwhelmed or found yourself slipping back into toxic patterns. Was it during a high-pressure period at work? Or perhaps interactions with someone in particular that left you emotionally drained? Recognizing these triggers is the first step in preventing them from overpowering you. Next, document these triggers in your plan, making them as specific as possible to avoid any ambiguity when stress hits.

Once your triggers are mapped out, the next phase involves listing down the coping strategies that have proven effective *for you* in the past that helped redirect your focus and alleviate stress. Make sure that these strategies are actionable and tailored to fit your lifestyle, ensuring they can be implemented whenever needed. For example, if one of your triggers is work-related stress, a coping strategy might involve taking scheduled breaks where you consciously step away from your workspace to engage in a brief meditation or a quick walk outside.

An essential component of your emotional safety plan is your support network. This network should comprise individuals who are supportive and understanding—people you can rely on to offer encouragement and sound advice when you're struggling. Include their contact information in your plan and outline how and when you might reach out to them during difficult times. Whether it's a family member, a close friend, or a therapist, knowing who you can turn to for support can make a significant difference in navigating emotional challenges.

Accessibility is key to the effectiveness of your emotional safety plan. Keep it in a format that is easy for you to access and review—whether that's a digital document on your smart-phone, a small notebook you carry with you, or a file on your computer. The easier it is to access, the more likely you are to utilize it when you feel your emotional stability is at risk. This accessibility ensures that no matter where you are or what situation you find yourself in, your plan is just a few seconds away, offering guidance and grounding you back to a state of emotional equilibrium.

Finally, the dynamic nature of life means that your emotional safety plan is not a static document—it should evolve as you do by updating your plan to reflect new insights, strategies, and changes in your support network regularly. Set a reminder, if necessary, to review and revise your plan periodically—be it monthly or quarterly. This regular update not only helps keep your plan relevant and effective but also reinforces your commitment to maintaining your emotional health.

Creating this personalized emotional safety plan will equip you with the map that will help you navigate through the "ups and downs" in your life with confidence and grace.

In the next chapter, we will explore additional strategies to enhance emotional resilience, further empowering you to lead a life characterized by emotional strength and stability.

EMPOWERING YOUR JOURNEY FORWARD

*A*s you work on yourself to overcome toxic emotion, remember that what you become in the future closely relies on your choices and actions. In this chapter, we focus on crafting your personal growth plan which will be a blueprint that will guide you in sculpting a future rich with achievement and emotional health.

CRAFTING YOUR PERSONAL GROWTH PLAN

The creation of a personal growth plan will aid in the fulfillment and joy you derive from living a life aligned with your deepest values and aspirations. The importance of having a structured plan is to prevent drifting aimlessly or get swayed by life's transient challenges and distractions.

Outline the Importance of a Personalized Plan

A personalized growth plan should be tailored to fit your unique psychological state, circumstances, and goals. It takes into account your strengths, weaknesses, opportunities, and threats—a strategy often encapsulated in the business world as SWOT analysis but equally applicable to personal development. By understanding these dynamics, you can create a plan that not only challenges you to grow but also leverages your innate abilities and aligns with your personal values. This alignment is crucial as it enhances not only the effectiveness of the plan but also your motivation to adhere to it, knowing that each step brings you closer to a version of yourself that you aspire to be.

Guide on Setting Realistic and Measurable Goals

Setting goals is an art that balances ambition with achievability. The SMART criteria streamline this process, ensuring that your goals are Specific, Measurable, Achievable, Relevant, and Time-bound. For instance, rather than setting a vague goal like "improve health," a SMART goal would be "to run a 5K in 30 minutes within six months by training three times a week." This specificity makes the goal more tangible, the progress measurable, and the target achievable within a set timeframe. It's also relevant to your broader aim of improving health. By breaking down your objectives in this manner, you transform the nebulous into the concrete, making your aspirations attainable one step at a time.

Incorporate Holistic Growth Aspects

Personal growth is multifaceted, encompassing emotional, social, professional, and physical dimensions. Your plan should, therefore, be holistic—addressing each of these areas. Emotional growth might involve practices like mindfulness or therapy sessions to enhance emotional intelligence. Social growth could focus on building or nurturing relationships and expanding your social network. Professional growth may include career planning, acquiring new skills, or advancing your educational qualifications. Physical growth covers aspects of health and fitness, dietary habits, and sleep. Integrating these varied aspects into your growth plan ensures a balanced approach to personal development, each facet supporting and enhancing the others.

Offer Templates and Tools for Plan Creation

To aid in this elaborate yet exciting task of plan creation, there are various templates and digital tools available. These resources provide a structured format that you can customize according to your specific goals and needs. For instance, a digital goal-setting template can help you outline your objectives, set deadlines, and track progress. Additionally, apps that focus on habit formation can be invaluable in maintaining the daily activities that contribute to your long-term goals. By utilizing these tools, you simplify the process of monitoring and adjusting your plan, ensuring that it remains responsive to your evolving aspirations and life circumstances.

In crafting your personal growth plan, you are essentially plotting the trajectory of your future self. This plan is not just a schedule of activities but a reflection of your commitment to live intentionally and purposefully. It's a statement that you are not leaving your development to chance, but rather taking proactive steps to mold and shape your destiny. As you engage with this planning process, remember that it is iterative. Life will change, and so will your goals and needs. The true power of your personal growth plan lies not just in its initial creation but in its ongoing adaptation—an ever-evolving blueprint that grows with you, ensuring that no matter the circumstances, you are ready to meet them with confidence and clarity.

THE ROLE OF COMMUNITY AND SUPPORT GROUPS IN HEALING

Each person's story is a thread in the tapestry of life, connecting us all in a supportive network. This aptly describes the role that community and support groups play in our lives, especially during times of personal growth and healing. Engaging with communities that resonate with your experiences and values can provide a scaffold of emotional support, significantly diminishing feelings of isolation that often accompany periods of stress or change. These groups offer not just support, but also diverse perspectives and shared experiences that can enrich your understanding and enhance your own coping strategies.

The benefits of such involvement are manifold. First, the emotional support provided by these communities can be a lifeline during tough times. Knowing you are not alone in your struggles can be incredibly reassuring; it validates your feelings and challenges, making them easier to navigate. Moreover, these groups often provide a safe space to express your feelings and fears without judgment, fostering an environment of acceptance and understanding. This feeling of belonging can boost your mental health significantly, reducing the risk of depression and anxiety.

Another advantage is the reduction of isolation. Modern life, with its rapid pace and often digital interactions, can lead to feelings of loneliness and detachment. Support groups counteract this by fostering a sense of community and connection. Shared experiences in these groups can also offer new insights and strategies for dealing with personal issues, provided by individuals who have faced similar challenges. This exchange of knowledge is invaluable as it broadens your understanding of your own experiences and introduces new methods of coping that may be more effective.

Finding the right group is important to gaining these benefits, and the process should be approached with thoughtfulness and intention. Start by identifying what you need from a support group. Are you looking for emotional support, practical advice, or both? What specific issues are you hoping to address, and are there groups that specialize in these areas? Once you have a clear understanding of your needs, you can begin searching for groups that meet these criteria. Many organizations and therapists can provide recommendations, and online resources can also be helpful. Websites that specialize in mental health resources can direct you to support groups for everything from depression and anxiety to specific life challenges like bereavement or divorce.

When you find a potential group, try attending a few sessions to see how you feel about the group's dynamics and the facilitation style. The right group should make you feel safe, respected, and understood. It should be a place where you can speak freely and where the feedback and interactions are constructive and supportive. Remember, the goal is not just to attend but to actively participate. Engaging fully in the group's activities and discussions maximizes the benefits you receive and contributes to the support of others in the group.

The choice between online and in-person support groups is another consideration that significantly affects your experience. Each format has its benefits and challenges. Online groups offer greater accessibility and convenience, especially for those with busy schedules or limited mobility. They can also provide anonymity, which might be comforting to those who are hesitant to share personal experiences face-to-face. However, online interactions can sometimes lack the depth and warmth of face-to-face communication, which can be crucial for emotional connection and support.

In-person groups, on the other hand, offer a level of personal interaction that can be more comforting and immediate. The physical presence of others sharing similar experiences can strengthen the sense of community and mutual support. However, these groups can be harder to attend regularly due to logistical issues such as location, timing, and transportation.

In deciding which format works best for you, consider your personal preferences, needs, and practical circumstances. Some find a hybrid approach beneficial—participating in both online and in-person groups to maximize the benefits of each. Whatever your choice, the key is consistency. Regular participation builds relationships and enhances the sense of community and support, which are essential for effective healing and growth.

As you continue to engage with your chosen support group, remember that the strength of a community lies not just in the support it offers you, but also in the support you extend to others. This reciprocal relationship enriches the group dynamic and amplifies the collective healing power of the community, making it a foundational element of your emotional well-being and personal growth.

LEVERAGING TECHNOLOGY FOR EMOTIONAL WELL-BEING

In an era where our daily lives are intertwined with digital interactions, it's important to recognize and use the tools that enhance our mental health. Think of your smartphone, often criticized for its role in increasing stress and distraction, as a potential ally in your emotional well-being. This device, when equipped with the right applications, can transform into a resource for mindfulness, emotional regulation, and therapy. Let's explore the digital tools designed to support mental health—mindfulness apps, mood trackers, and therapy platforms—and discuss how these can be integrated effectively into your life to foster emotional wellness.

Relevant digital tools have flourished, offering functionalities that range from guided meditation and breathing exercises to comprehensive mood tracking and virtual therapy sessions. Mindfulness apps like "Headspace," "Balanced: Medication & Sleep," and "Calm" provide guided meditations that help reduce anxiety and improve concentration. These apps often feature a variety of sessions on topics such as sleep, anxiety, and focus, making them versatile tools in managing daily stressors. Mood trackers, such as "Daylio," allow you to record your emotional states throughout the day, helping you identify patterns or triggers in your mood fluctuations. This can be incredibly insightful, particularly when trying to establish connections between your activities and emotional responses. Therapy apps like "Talkspace" and "BetterHelp" offer access to professional counseling services through your phone, making mental health support accessible without the need to travel to a therapist's office.

The advantages of using technology in managing mental health are significant. These tools provide accessible, customizable, and often cost-effective alternatives or supplements to traditional mental health therapies. Accessibility is perhaps the most evident benefit, as these apps and platforms bring mental health resources right to your fingertips, anytime and anywhere. This can be particularly life-changing for individuals in remote or underserved areas where mental health services are scarce or nonexistent. Furthermore, the customizable nature of digital mental health tools means that you can often tailor the experience to fit your personal preferences and needs, whether it's choosing a meditation length that fits your schedule or selecting a therapist who specializes in the issues you're facing.

When choosing technological tools to aid in your mental health journey, it's crucial to consider several factors to ensure their effectiveness and reliability by examining user reviews and ratings on the app store. Privacy policies are another critical area to review; ensure that the app or platform has robust security measures to protect your personal and sensitive data. Look for apps developed by credible organizations or individuals with expertise in mental health. For therapy apps, check the qualifications and licensure of the therapists involved to ensure you are receiving professional and ethical care.

While the benefits of digital tools for mental health are manifold, it is essential to maintain a balanced approach to their use. It's easy to become overly reliant on these tools, potentially leading to a form of digital overload where your screen time significantly increases, which can paradoxically contribute to stress and anxiety. To avoid this, it's advisable to integrate these digital practices with offline activities that promote mental health. Physical exercise, face-to-face interactions with friends and family, and engaging in hobbies that do not involve screens are vital components of a well-rounded mental health strategy. Balancing online and offline activities helps ensure that your engagement with digital tools remains healthy and beneficial, enhancing your overall well-being without leading to burnout or overdependence on technology.

Incorporating technology into your emotional well-being strategy offers a modern solution to the age-old quest for inner peace and emotional stability. By judiciously selecting and utilizing these digital tools, you empower yourself with additional resources to manage your mental health effectively, ensuring that you remain resilient in the face of life's challenges.

CELEBRATING MILESTONES IN YOUR EMOTIONAL RECOVERY JOURNEY

Recognizing and celebrating milestones in your emotional recovery journey are not just acts of self-congratulation but essential components of the healing process. Each milestone achieved is like a beacon on a hill, illuminating your path and reminding you of how far you've come from the shadows of your past struggles. Celebrating these achievements does more than just mark progress; it boosts your morale, reinforces the positive changes you've made, and fuels your motivation to continue forward. Imagine finally running that half-marathon after months of training or realizing it's been a year since your last panic attack—these are significant victories that deserve recognition and celebration.

Suggest Ways to Celebrate Achievements

When it comes to celebrating these milestones, the key is to create memorable and meaningful experiences that resonate with the personal significance of your achievements. One heartfelt way to celebrate is by sharing your successes with loved ones. Organizing a small gathering or dinner where you can share the hurdles you've overcome. Loved ones often want to celebrate your successes as much as you do, and sharing these moments can deepen your relationships and provide mutual joy.

Another creative way to commemorate these milestones is by treating yourself to a special experience that aligns with your interests and passions. For instance, if you've successfully managed to reduce your anxiety through meditation, perhaps a weekend retreat could both celebrate your progress and enhance your practice. Alternatively, creating a visual representation of your progress, such as a photo collage or a custom journal, can provide a tangible reminder of your journey and a source of inspiration during challenging times.

Encourage Reflection During Celebrations

While celebrations can be joyous and exhilarating, integrating reflective practices into these occasions can magnify their impact, turning them into profound learning experiences. Take time during your celebrations to reflect on the journey that brought you to this point. What were the challenges? What strategies proved most effective to you? How have you grown through these experiences? This reflection not only provides a deeper appreciation of your accomplishments but also helps you strategize for future challenges. It ensures that each milestone isn't just a checkmark on a list but a stepping stone in a continuous journey of self-improvement and understanding.

Promote Gratitude Practices

Incorporating gratitude into your celebrations can significantly enhance the emotional richness of these moments. Gratitude shifts your focus from what's missing to what's present, amplifying the positive aspects of your life and increasing your overall life satisfaction. After acknowledging your own efforts and achievements, take a moment to express gratitude for the support and opportunities that facilitated your progress. Whether it's thanking a therapist, a friend, or even your own resilience, acknowledging the help you received can deepen your sense of connection to those around you and to your own journey. Practicing gratitude not only during celebrations but as a daily ritual can create a pervasive sense of contentment and fortitude, reinforcing your emotional resilience.

In celebrating your milestones, you not only honor your past efforts but also prepare yourself for the road ahead. Each celebration is a reaffirmation of your ability to overcome challenges and a reinforcement of your commitment to personal growth. As you continue to navigate the complexities of life, let these celebrations be your milestones, not just of where you have been, but of the heights you are still to achieve.

EMPOWERING OTHERS: SHARING YOUR JOURNEY TO INSPIRE

In a previous chapter, we mentioned the importance of participating in support groups. When you share your personal experiences, particularly those involving overcoming challenges or personal growth, you do much more than recount events; you illuminate pathways for others and validate their struggles and aspirations. This act of sharing can profoundly impact both the teller and the listener. It creates a unique space where understanding and empathy flourish, and collective wisdom grows. For the storyteller, articulating your story is not just about narrating events; it's an opportunity to reflect on your growth, which can reinforce your own learning and emotional resilience. For the listener, your story provides hope and potentially a roadmap for navigating similar challenges.

Sharing your experiences can be incredibly empowering. It converts personal struggles and victories into communal resources, enabling others to feel less alone in their journeys. This sense of solidarity is potent and can foster a supportive community atmosphere where people feel safe to express their vulnerabilities and share their strengths. Furthermore, when you share your story, you contribute to a larger narrative of human experience and resilience, which can be incredibly affirming. It validates not only your path but also the universal struggle against and triumph over life's adversities.

However, sharing personal stories must be done thoughtfully and respectfully, considering both your own privacy and the emotional impact on your audience. Begin by deciding how much of your story you are comfortable sharing—set clear boundaries about what is and isn't shared. It's essential to consider the context in which you're sharing your story, whether it's a public blog post, a podcast, or a more intimate setting like a support group meeting. Each platform has different implications for privacy and audience interaction, and choosing the right platform can affect how your message is received and processed.

For instance, if you're considering a blog or a podcast as your medium, plan your narrative structure carefully. Start with outlining the key moments you wish to share, then consider how to present these moments in a way that is both engaging and sensitive. It's often helpful to focus on the emotions and lessons learned rather than just the events. This approach not only makes your story more relatable but also more inspiring. It shifts the narrative from a series of events to a journey of emotional growth and discovery.

Furthermore, when sharing in digital formats like blogs or podcasts, it's wise to anticipate and prepare for public feedback. Online platforms can expose you to a wide audience, which includes varying opinions and reactions. Establishing a way to manage comments—deciding whether to respond to them, and if so, how—can help maintain a healthy dialogue and protect your emotional well-being.

Conferences and social media platforms also offer significant opportunities to share your story and inspire others. Speaking at a conference can be particularly impactful because it allows for direct engagement with an audience, providing an immediate feedback loop that can be incredibly validating. When preparing for such opportunities, practice your speech thoroughly and focus on conveying your message clearly and confidently. Social media platforms, meanwhile, can help reach a broader audience. Platforms like Instagram or Facebook allow for multimedia storytelling, combining text, images, and videos to create a compelling narrative. When using social media, consider the visual elements of your story—images that represent moments of challenge or triumph can enhance your message and engage your audience more deeply.

In fostering this culture of sharing and support, you not only aid others in their personal growth but also reinforce your own progress. This creates a positive feedback loop where helping others improves your own emotional resilience, affirming the value of your experiences and your recovery. Each act of sharing becomes a step in reinforcing your own journey and contributing to a broader narrative of healing and growth.

In this interconnected world, your story has the power to not only reflect your past but also to forge connections and build futures—not just your own, but also those of others who find solace, inspiration, and practical guidance in your words. By opening up to others about your challenges and victories, you participate in a collective journey of healing, learning, and growing together.

In summary, this chapter has explored the transformative power of sharing your personal journey and the positive impacts it can have on both yourself and others. By choosing appropriate platforms, setting boundaries, and engaging thoughtfully, you can turn your personal narrative into a powerful tool for communal healing and inspiration.

CONCLUSION

As you read "Toxic No More," it's important to reflect on the ground you have covered. You have navigated a transformative path, from the initial steps of recognizing and understanding the pervasive nature of toxic emotions and relationships, to adopting strategies for self-protection and ultimately, empowering yourself for continuous growth and healthy relational dynamics.

The cornerstone of this journey has been the relentless commitment to self-awareness and self-compassion. Remember, overcoming toxic emotions is not a finite destination but a continuous voyage of discovery, learning, and adaptation. Each chapter of this book has equipped you with knowledge and practical tools, but the true essence lies in applying these strategies consistently in your daily life.

The role of community and support systems and the practical application of the strategies and tools we have discussed is crucial. Use the templates, participate in the exercises, and leverage the digital resources provided to actively engage in your journey towards emotional wellness. These are not merely suggestions but implements in your toolkit for building a healthier, more fulfilled life. Stay open to continuous learning, follow newsletters, and keep in touch with thought leaders in the field to ensure that your strategies for well-being are informed and current.

Let us take a moment to celebrate your progress and resilience. Engaging with this book and starting on this path requires courage—a testament to your strength and dedication. Remember, *every small step forward is a victory*, a push against the tide of toxicity towards a shore of emotional freedom and stability.

Finally, I leave you with a message of hope and empowerment. Healing and growth are within your reach, achievable for everyone, including you. Embrace the journey with an open heart and mind. You are not alone, and you possess the strength to transform your life from toxic to thriving.

Together, we can foster a world where emotional well-being is not just a possibility but a reality for all. Keep moving forward, keep growing, and know that in your journey to reclaim your life, you are a beacon of hope and strength. Thank you for taking this journey with me. Let's continue to thrive, inspire, and transform, one step at a time.

I APPRECIATE YOUR REVIEW

Customer Reviews

★★★★★ 2
5.0 out of 5 stars ▾

5 star	100%
4 star	0%
3 star	0%
2 star	0%
1 star	0%

See all verified purchase reviews ·

Share your thoughts with other customers

Write a customer review

I would be incredibly thankful if you take just
60-seconds to write a brief review on Amazon,
even if it's just a few sentences!

https://amazon.com/review/create-review?asin=1960188364

ABOUT THE AUTHOR

Janet G. Cruz

With a robust academic foundation in Sociology and Psychology, Janet is deeply passionate about understanding the complexities of human behavior. Her expertise lies particularly in the realm of addiction, where she have authored several insightful books that delve into various types of dependency. These works aim not only to educate but also to offer practical strategies for overcoming addiction. Her goal is to contribute meaningfully to public awareness on issues related to mental health and societal well-being.

By leveraging her comprehensive knowledge and experience, she strives to foster a more informed and compassionate approach towards individuals struggling with addiction.

She has also worked in the healthcare industry for many years and has firsthand experience with the challenges associated with caring for a loved one with dementia and more.

Her passion to help others led her to write a series of books on dementia caregiving; a series of comprehensive resources for family and friends of those living with dementia.

Janet is a passionate voice for dementia caregiving and about giving those who are caring for someone with dementia the support and resources needed to ensure their loved one can live a safe, comfortable, and dignified life.

She expertly blends scientific insight with personal narration to offer readers a comprehensive understanding of the relationship between addiction, the brain, and recovery.

Her mission is to help others find hope, strength, and solace in their journey. With her work, the author hopes to reduce the isolation and stresses associated with addiction.

She is the author of a variety of books in English and Spanish, such as The Dementia Caregiver's Guide,Dementia Caregiving, Guía de Supervivencia para Cuidadores de Personas con Demencia, ""The Power of Communication Skills and Effective Listening: Say What You Mean and Mean What You Say"", and "Developing Drug Addiction Recovery Skills by Understanding Addiction and The Brain: The Ultimate Guide to Build Resilience to Prevent Relapse," also available in Spanish, and many other books.

BIBLIOGRAPHY

"Negative emotions." Better Health Channel . https://www.betterhealth.vic.gov.au/health/healthyliving/negative-emotions

"Chronic Stress Can Hurt Your Overall Health." ColumbiaDoctors. 2023-05-19. https://www.columbiadoctors.org/news/chronic-stress-can-hurt-your-overall-health

Butler, Rachel M; Boden; Matthew T, Olino, Thomas M; Morrison, Amanda S.; Golden, Philippe R.; Gross, James J. and Heimberg, Richard G. *"Emotional Clarity and Attention to Emotions in Cognitive Behavioral Group Therapy and Mindfulness-Based Stress Reduction for Social Anxiety Disorder."* National Library of Medicine. 2019. https://www.ncbi.nlm.nih.gov/pmc/articles/PMC3887268/

"Adverse childhood experiences: impacts on adult mental." PubMed Centra. 2023-10-23. https://www.ncbi.nlm.nih.gov/pmc/articles/PMC10639139/

Elizabeth Scott, PhD. *"What to KNOW about if You're Concerned About a Toxic Relationship."* Veriwellmind. 2023-11-03. https://www.verywellmind.com/toxic-relationships-4174665

Rachel Mall, MSN. *"What are the long-term effects of gaslighting."* MedicalNewsToday. 2020-06-20. https://www.medicalnewstoday.com/articles/long-term-effects-of-gaslighting

Daniella Beer-Becker, Psychologist. *"How to Overcome Emotional Dependency."* BlakePsychology. 2022-03-01. https://www.blakepsychology.com/2022/03/how-to-overcome-emotional-dependency/

"How to Set Boundaries With a Difficult Family Member." New York Times. 2023-03-08. https://www.nytimes.com/2023/03/08/well/family/boundaries-family-nedra-glover-tawwab.html

Sheldon Reid. *"Setting Healthy Boundaries in Relationships."* HelpGuide. https://www.helpguide.org/articles/relationships-communication/setting-healthy-boundaries-in-relationships.htm

Kira M Newman. *"Five Science-Backed Strategies to Build Resilience."* Greater Good Magazine. 2016-11-09. https://greatergood.berkeley.edu/article/item/five_science_backed_strategies_to_build_resilience

"Mindfulness for Your Health." News in Health. 2021-06. https://newsinhealth. nih.gov/2021/06/mindfulness-your-health

Seraine Page. *"Affirmations and Mental Health: Does Positive Talk Help Well-Being?"* TotalWellnessHealth. 2022-07-21. https://info.totalwellnesshealth. com/blog/affirmations-and-mental-health

Elizabeth Scott, PhD. *"Assertive Communication: What It Means and How to Use It."* VeryWellMind. 2023-09-26. https://www.verywellmind.com/learn-assertive-communication-in-five-simple-steps-3144969

"How to Change Your Mindset and Say No Without Feeling Guilt." Course Correction Coaching. https://www.coursecorrectioncoaching.com/say-no-with out-feeling-guilt/

"50 Ways to Do Digital Detox Every Day." Westgate Resorts. 2024-01-03. https:// www.westgateresorts.com/blog/ways-to-digital-detox/

Dr. Chris Mosunic, PhD, RD, CDCES, MBA. *"How to create a self-care plan person-alized to your needs."* Calm. https://www.calm.com/blog/self-care-plan

Crystal Raypole. *"30 Grounding Techniques to Quiet Distressing Thoughts."* HealthLine. 2024-01-29. https://www.healthline.com/health/grounding-techniques

"Coping with stress at work." American Psychology Association. 2014-07-01. https://www.apa.org/topics/healthy-workplaces/work-stress

Amy Morin of Inc. *"5 Strategies Resilient People Use to Overcome Rejection (No Matter How Much it Stings)."* The Muse. 2020-06-19. https://www.themuse. com/advice/5-strategies-resilient-people-use-to-overcome-rejection-no-matter-how-much-it-stings

J. Douglas Bremner, MD. *"Traumatic stress: effects on the brain - PMC."* National Library of Medicine. 2006-12. https://www.ncbi.nlm.nih.gov/pmc/articles/ PMC3181836/

Thomas Blake. *"Unlocking Healing: The Success of EMDR Therapy."* Thomas Blake Therapy. https://www.thomasblaketherapy.com/blog/unlocking-healing-the-success-of-emdr-therapy

Courtney Ackerman, MA. *"19 Best Narrative Therapy Techniques & Worksheets [+PDF]"* PositivePsychology. 2017-06-18. https://positivepsychology.com/ narrative-therapy/

Philip H. Friedman, Ph.D. *"Healing from Anxiety, Depression, Trauma Using Forgiveness, Self-Compassion, and Energy Psychology while Tracking Change Over Time."* Society for the Advancement of Psychotherapy. 2019-06-12. https://societyforpsychotherapy.org/healing-from-anxiety-depression-trauma-using-forgiveness-self-compassion-and-energy-psychology-while-tracking-change-over-time-2/

Antonio Crego, Jose Ramón Yela, Pablo Riesco-Matías, Maria-Angeles Gómez-Martínez, and Aitor Vicente-Arruebarrena. *"The Benefits of Self-Compassion in Mental Health Professionals: A Systematic Review of Empirical Research."* National Library of Medicine, Psychology Res Behave Manag. 2022-09-22. https://www.ncbi.nlm.nih.gov/pmc/articles/PMC9482966/

Jo Nash, Ph.D. *"Fostering Self-Forgiveness: 25 Powerful Techniques and Books."* PositivePsychology. 2021-07-05. https://positivepsychology.com/self-forgiveness/

"Forgiveness: Letting go of grudges and bitterness." Mayo Clinic. 2022-11-22. https://www.mayoclinic.org/healthy-lifestyle/adult-health/in-depth/forgiveness/art-20047692

Dr. Chris Mosunic, PhD, RD, CDES, MBA. *"Negative self-talk: 8 ways to quiet your inner critic."* Calm Blog. https://www.calm.com/blog/negative-self-talk

Andrea Bonior, Ph.D. *"What Does a Healthy Relationship Look Like?"* Psychology Today. 2018-12-28. https://www.psychologytoday.com/us/blog/friendship-20/201812/what-does-healthy-relationship-look

Lawrence Robinson, Jeanne Segal, Ph.D., and Melinda Smith, M.A. *"Effective Communication: Improving Your Interpersonal Skills"* HelpGuide. 2024-05-08. https://www.helpguide.org/articles/relationships-communication/effective-communication.htm

Joe Sanok. *"A Guide to Setting Better Boundaries."* Harvard Business Review. 2022-04-14. https://hbr.org/2022/04/a-guide-to-setting-better-boundaries

Lawrence Robinson, Melinda Smith, M.A., and Jeanne Segal, Ph.D. *"Tips for Building a Healthy Relationship."* HelpGuide. 2024-04-10. https://www.helpguide.org/articles/relationships-communication/relationship-help.htm

Kendra Cherry, MSEd. *"Signs That You're In an Unhealthy Relationship."* VeryWellMind. 2023-11-09. https://www.verywellmind.com/signs-that-youre-in-an-unhealthy-relationship-5218237

Simón Guendelman, Sebastián Medeiros, and Hagen Rampes. *"Mindfulness and Emotional Regulation: Insights from Neurological, Psychological, and Clinical Studies."* National Library of Medicine - Front Psychol. 2017-03-06. https://www.ncbi.nlm.nih.gov/pmc/articles/PMC5337506/

Aditya Mahindru, Pradeep Patil, and Tarun Agrawal. *"Role of Physical Activity on Mental Health and Well-Being: A Review."* National Library of Medicine -

Cureus. 2023-01-15. https://www.ncbi.nlm.nih.gov/pmc/articles/PMC9902068/

"*Emotional Safety Planning.*" National Domestic Violence Hotline https://www.thehotline.org/resources/emotional-safety-planning/

Scott Jeffrey. "*How to Craft a Personal Development Plan that Inspires Meaningful, Long-Term Results.*" CEOsage. 2024-04-10. https://scottjeffrey.com/personal-development-plan/

Toni Hoy. "*Support Groups: Types, Benefits, and What to Expect.*" HelpGuide. https://www.helpguide.org/articles/therapy-medication/support-groups.htm

Laura Dorwart. "*10 Best Mental Health and Therapy Apps.*" VeryWell. 2024-03-22. https://www.verywellmind.com/best-mental-health-apps-4692902

"*Why Celebrating Addiction Recovery Milestones is Important.*" BOLD Health. 2024-03-27. https://boldhealthinc.com/celebrating-addiction-recovery-milestones/

www.ingramcontent.com/pod-product-compliance
Lightning Source LLC
Chambersburg PA
CBHW071405120626
46546CB00002B/825